Enigma Books

Also published by Enigma Books

Hitler's Table Talk: 1941–1944
In Stalin's Secret Service
Hitler and Mussolini: The Secret Meetings
The Jews in Fascist Italy: A History
The Man Behind the Rosenbergs
Roosevelt and Hopkins: An Intimate History
Diary 1937–1943 (Galeazzo Ciano)
Secret Affairs: FDR, Cordell Hull, and Sumner Welles
Hitler and His Generals: Military Conferences 1942–1945
Stalin and the Jews: The Red Book
The Secret Front: Nazi Political Espionage
Fighting the Nazis: French Intelligence and Counterintelligence
A Death in Washington: Walter G. Krivitsky and the Stalin Terror
The Battle of the Casbah: Terrorism and Counterterrorism in Algeria 1955–1957
Hitler's Second Book: The Unpublished Sequel to *Mein Kampf*
At Napoleon's Side in Russia: The Classic Eyewitness Account
The Atlantic Wall: Hitler's Defenses for D-Day
Double Lives: Stalin, Willi Münzenberg and the Seduction of the Intellectuals
France and the Nazi Threat: The Collapse of French Diplomacy 1932–1939
Mussolini: The Secrets of His Death
Top Nazi: Karl Wolff—The Man Between Hitler and Himmler
Empire on the Adriatic: Mussolini's Conquest of Yugoslavia
The Origins of the War of 1914 (3-volume set)
Hitler's Foreign Policy: 1933–1939. The Road to World War II
The Origins of Fascist Ideology 1918–1925
Max Corvo: OSS Italy 1942–1945
Hitler's Contract: The Secret History of the Italian Edition of *Mein Kampf*
Secret Intelligence and the Holocaust
Israel at High Noon
Balkan Inferno: Betrayal, War, and Intervention, 1990–2005
Hollywood's Celebrity Gangster
Calculated Risk
The Murder of Maxim Gorky
The Kravchenko Case

Ezio Costanzo

The Mafia and the Allies

Sicily 1943
and the Return of the Mafia

Enigma Books

Enigma Books
580 Eighth Avenue, New York, NY 10018
www.enigmabooks.com

Originally published in Italian under the title
Mafia & Alleati
Servizi segreti americani e sbarco in Sicilia.
Da Lucky Luciano ai sindaci uomini d'onore
By Le Nove Muse – Tiziana Guerrera, Catania

First U.S. Edition

Copyright © 2007 Enigma Books

All photos in this book come from the author's collection.

Translated by George Lawrence

ISBN 978-1-929631-68-1

Printed in the United States of America

Library of Congress Cataloging-in-Publication Data

Costanzo, Ezio.
  [Mafia & alleati. English]
  The Mafia and the Allies : Sicily 1943, the return of the Mafia / Ezio Costanzo ; translated by George Lawrence. -- 1st U.S. ed.

    p. : ill. ; cm.

  Includes bibliographical references and index.
  Translation of: Mafia & alleati : servizi segreti americani e sbarco in Sicilia : da Lucky Luciano ai sindaci uomini d'onore.
  ISBN: 978-1-929631-68-1

1. World War, 1939-1945--Secret service--United States. 2. Mafia--United States. 3. Mafia--Italy--Sicily. 4. World War, 1939-1945--Campaigns--Italy--Sicily. 5. United States. Office of Naval Intelligence. 6. Sicily(Italy)--History--1870-1945. I. Lawrence, George. (George Wilson) II. Title. III. Title: Mafia & alleati.

D810.S7 C6713 2007
940.54

Ezio Costanzo

A newsman and writer, Ezio Costanzo has been active in historical research on the Second World War for many years. He has worked at the National Archives in Washington D.C. and specializes in the history of the Anglo-American occupation of Italy. He is also a professor of radio and television arts at the University of Palermo. Among his other books: *I bambini e la guerra* (with Aldo Forbice, edizione Rai Eri, Unicef Le Nove Muse 2005); *Sicilia 1943. Breve storia dello sbarco alleato* (Le Nove Muse, 2003) he is also the author and director of the documentary film: *Sicilia 1943*. Ezio Costanzo lives and works in Catania.

Contents

Preface

This book tells the story of events that took place from 1941 to 1943 when the main protagonists were the bosses of the American Mafia, the Sicilian "Godfathers," and the intelligence services of the United States. The 1954 investigation by New York State Commissioner of Investigations Judge William Herlands and recently declassified documents from archives located in the United States allow us to clarify the myriad pieces of information and subsequent denials that this controversial issue has created over the last few years.

Lucky Luciano, Calogero Vizzini, OSS officers Max Corvo and Vincent Scamporino, the head of the AMG Colonel Charles Poletti, and many others are the characters that fill the pages of this book. The backdrop is provided by Operation Husky, the Anglo-American occupation of Sicily. An imposing set of intelligence operations was put together by the United States, including secret operatives representing various military and political agencies involved in collecting information about the island among Sicilians residing in the United States, and later on for a series of operations on the ground in the wake of the advancing armies.

Contrary to the usual perceptions, Sicily turned out to be a poor testing ground for most of those agents and many espionage operations were to fail because of the lack of coordination among the intelligence services and the military. A few documents from the OSS (Office of Strategic Services) will provide a useful cross-check of the period immediately following the occupation of Sicily and the Allied administration of the island; the documents proving that the covert intervention by the United States government in Italian internal affairs went beyond the legitimate and sincere spirit of freedom and democracy to influence the political and economic choices of the nation, including those intended to prevent a Communist victory during the first postwar elections. The alliance with the conservative elements on the island brokered by the Mafia was useful to the Allies, not only to administer Sicily while they were there but even more to lay the foundations of the social and political future of an Italy without the Communists who were under attack by both liberals and Catholics as well as by the Mafiosi. Following the American landings and for the first time in its history, the Mafia was allowed to appear as a legitimate political and administrative organization protected by an army of occupation. The old godfathers were able to combine their strong traditions with the prestige of being protected by the new conquerors.

In 1974 the Italian parliamentary commission of inquiry into the Mafia problem in Sicily attempted to secure an important historical document. On June 20 Senator Luigi Carraro, who headed the Commission, asked Minister of Foreign Affairs Aldo Moro to provide a document that was still secret, listing the names of the many Mafiosi who had collaborated with U.S. Intelligence in the planning of the landings in Sicily in 1943. Sen. Carraro wrote to the minister stating that the document was "attached to Article 16 of the armistice treaty of 1943 between Italy and the Allied Powers," which mentioned an agreement between the Allies and the Mafia giving the Mafiosi, in exchange for their help, complete impunity and forgiving any and all criminal acts perpetrated before the Anglo-American forces occupied the island. Carraro asked Moro to undertake a series of investigations to locate that valuable document in the archives of the Farnesina (the Italian Ministry of Foreign Affairs). The minister ordered the search but no trace of the list could be found. A letter was sent out two months later stating: "Following the requested research among the available documents in the archives of this ministry we have been unable to confirm with any precision the existence of a document as described. It does not appear as an attachment of the short armistice [the document signed at Cassibile on September 3, 1943] nor the so-called long armistice [with additional conditions in the instrument of surrender that Italy signed in Malta on September 29, 1943]." Moro further stated that "the short armistice that included 12 articles contained only military points and that the long armistice that included 44 articles had no language that alluded to the issue as requested. We therefore tend to conclude that the information requested is not accurate."

Moro's terse reply was ironic in several ways: the armistice signed on September 3 contained only 12 articles; there could therefore be no attachment to a nonexistent "article 16." Actually if the Commission was serious about finding that piece of paper containing the names of the Mafiosi having collaborated with secret American operatives they should have looked at the text of the peace treaty between Italy and the Allies signed in Paris on February 10, 1947. Article 16 of that treaty stated specifically that "Italy shall not indict or otherwise incriminate any Italian citizen, including those who were part of the armed forces, for having, during the time period from June 10, 1940, until the promulgation of this treaty, expressed sympathy or taken action in favor of the Allied and Associated Powers."

The purported existence of that list of names (some claim that there were at least 800) is not just a figment of someone's imagination, since these would have to be openly anti-Fascist individuals who had gone over to the Allied cause and had suffered persecution under the old dictatorship. The members of the Mafia could all make such claims. Of course besides the traditional members of the honored society who benefited from article 16 there were also many anti-Fascists and pro-American Sicilians who had switched sides at the eleventh hour.

Despite the attempt by the anti-Mafia Commission to secure the list of those who had been pardoned, no trace of that document could be found anywhere. The list of the Sicilian gangsters who had helped the intelligence services during the operations on the island provided by the head of Cosa Nostra, Charles "Lucky" Luciano, to US Naval Intelligence officers was also never found. This means therefore that in the absence of any documentary evidence, anything written on the subject shall remain purely speculative. It is also true that written documents on the topic showing any kind of agreement between any government and known criminals are also unlikely to be found. Certainly no contract between Mafia bosses and Roosevelt's intelligence organizations was ever put in writing. Mafia leaders were not in the habit of leaving behind any kind of paper trail and certainly no incriminating lists of names. However, the absence of corroborating evidence should not preclude the existence of such an agreement. The Americans may have used well-known Mafia experts to facilitate the conquest of Sicily and its governance but certainly did not need them to win any battles or prepare for military operations.

Two important American investigations of the 1950s well known to researchers were those of U.S. Senator Estes Kefauver on organized crime and its connections to politicians and businessmen, and that of Judge William Herlands, who also specifically investigated the contribution made by American mobsters to the war effort. Some very significant details have emerged regarding the daring way that the so-called Operation Underworld was successfully conducted. The accounts and memoirs of the main players prove beyond a doubt that an agreement in fact had to exist and that the American Mafia was key to guaranteeing the security of the ships bound for Europe and in the painstaking research of data in preparation of the occupation of Sicily.

Some scholars persist in referring to the issue as a "legend" or at best acknowledge that the Americans began with military considerations regarding administrative control of the occupied territories. In other words it was in fact an "unlucky" choice that led to the unplanned and unwelcome reorganization of Mafia power on the island. As Anthony Marsloe, the US Naval officer who landed in Sicily with General Patton, stated in one of his last interviews to the BBC in London:

> …we had to use any means to defend the United States and find help for what we were doing and were about to do…Were some of the people we contracted part of the Mafia? I couldn't care less what they were as long as they could provide any kind of information that could have helped the war effort.

Paul Alfieri, another US Navy agent, landed in Sicily the same day as Marsloe and offered the Herlands Commission a different interpretation of the relationship with the Mafia:

> ...in the overwhelming majority of the cases those contacts existed as the result of the collaboration of boss Lucky Luciano. That information proved to be rather useful.

This book was made possible thanks to the collaboration of many people. I thank Dr. Pappalardo and the personnel of the Archivio Storico della Commissione Nazionale Anti-mafia; Dr. Claudia Pennacchio of the Archivio Storico del Senato; the personnel of the documents and photographic section of the National Archives in Washington D.C.; Prof. Joseph Salemi at New York University; Dr. Rita Carbonaro, director of the Ursino-Recupero library in Catania; Dr. Anna Risicato of the library of the Facoltà di Economie Commercio in Catania.

I owe a special thanks to Bill Corvo, the son of Max Biagio Corvo, head of OSS Italy from 1943 to 1945, for his patient help and for the documents provided from the Max Corvo Archive in Middletown, Connecticut.

I thank Lucia Bruno and Daniela Caruso, who organized my archives; and Elvira Fusto for her invaluable suggestions; Salvy Bognanno; De Lise Vaccino; and Francesca Vitale.

Ezio Costanzo
Ragalna sull'Etna 2007

The Mafia and
the Allies

Chapter 1

The Landings in Sicily
and U. S. Intelligence

D-Day and H-Hour came in the early morning of July 10, 1943. The population of Sicily, however, was completely unaware that the largest amphibious operation of the Second World War, Operation Husky—the Anglo-American invasion and occupation of Sicily, the southernmost line of defense of Fascist Italy—had just begun. Three hours past midnight, soldiers of the American Third Division began landing on the beaches at Licata, taking the first step in the conquest of Nazi Europe.

An endless metal platform studded the sea's horizon, helped along by strong southwesterly winds that had been blowing all night. The people of Gela, Licata, Pachino, Marzamemi, and so many other small towns and villages overlooking the Mediterranean had gone to bed early to the distant and worrisome sounds of Italian and German anti-aircraft guns that troubled their sleep. There were actually some two thousand ships of all kinds filled with soldiers and weapons moving to the coast. Above some of the ships hovered cigar-shaped balloons intended to deflect any expected German air attacks. During the first three days 181,000 men, 1,800 pieces of artillery, 600 tanks, and 14,000 trucks and jeeps went ashore in Sicily. The U.S. Seventh Army and the British Eighth Army divided the sun-drenched territory: General George S. Patton's men went west while General Bernard Law Montgomery marched east. Neither of the two was allowed to overlap into the other's assigned territorial limits during the offensive. These battle plans had been agreed to six months before at the conference at Casablanca and had established that both armies could meet only during the final phase of the advance toward the city of Messina, which was the final objective that would have secured complete military control of the island. The hostility between the two Allied generals surfaced bitterly during the summer of 1943, to the extent that several tactical mistakes in operations were reported back to Eisenhower, who was in overall command of operations in the Mediterranean.

The battle for the conquest of Sicily lasted thirty-seven very long days, during which over 13,000 soldiers of both Allied and Axis armies died. Tons of bombs massacred the civilian population and the exact number of those killed was never ascertained. English and American pilots bombed the entire island, thereby enacting the lethal strategy of terror that Churchill and Roosevelt had agreed upon: a ruthless system intended to reduce enemy morale through an endless rain of fire that the British called "morale bombing," meant to prevent any kind of human reactions. Even though Allied military superiority was overwhelming, the Sicilian campaign left many British and American officers with a bitter taste in their mouth, mostly because of the vicious bickering between Patton and Montgomery. Both generals had underestimated the reaction of the Axis VIth Army of General Guzzoni, which included 175,000 Italians and 28,000 Germans, that in some parts of the island managed to delay the Allied offensive. At Primosole, a few kilometers outside Catania, the Germans were able to block General Montgomery for seventeen days during his advance toward the city under Mount Etna, while just north of Gela, during the first day of fighting, the Italian Livorno division managed to push Patton's men back to the sea before being cut to pieces by American naval artillery.

It is also true that in other parts of Sicily many Italian soldiers, sergeants, captains, and generals preferred to surrender and hand over their weapons to the enemy, quickly removing their uniforms to disguise themselves as peasants. At Siracusa, for example, where the imposing coastal battery was not engaged, Italian soldiers opted for mass flight toward the more secure flanks of Mount Etna; a surrender followed the general confusion of troops abandoned by their officers in the face of overwhelming odds, giving rise to various interpretations including the insinuation that the Italian surrender was the result of the pressures brought by the Mafia and U.S. intelligence. This explanation becomes even more plausible in view of the warm welcome given to Patton's army by the population as it advanced into Sicily. Newsreels show American GIs smiling as they march amid the populace that was waving white handkerchiefs and crying out "liberators!" They looked like a well organized, oddly cinematic crowd, perhaps a bit too spontaneous and friendly toward those tall young men chewing gum. It may not be outlandish to think that someone may have suggested to those bystanders how they should behave when their American cousins marched in and in fact suggested to the few Italian soldiers left to defend the mountains to simply return home since the war was over at last. At San Giuseppe Jato, near Palermo, the enthusiasm of the crowd came as a surprise even to *Life* magazine correspondent Jack Belden, who published a very long article on August 6, 1943.

Strange things have been happening around here. A column of armored personnel carriers, artillery, Sherman tanks, and jeeps had stopped in the middle of town. Young and old people on the gridiron balconies were screaming and waving white kerchiefs and pieces of cloth as though they were flags of happiness. You could hear the words "Good American." Young women were throwing flowers. The girls' hair flowing here and there as they blew kisses. The entire street seemed to be moving like a wave from one side to the other.

In Giacalone, another little village near Monreale, Belden saw most of the same things happening:

> ...behind the white sheets there was a crowd of poor malnourished people who clamored, yelled, clapped slowly at first and then harder... They were throwing watermelons and apricots on our jeep. There was excitement, noise, and commotion everywhere. A column of Italian soldiers were marching through the crowd on the side of the road with their hands held high over their heads... Another soldier walked and cried with tears running down his face. Those prisoners were looking in amazement at the people cheering the invaders that they had attempted to keep out of the village only a few minutes before. I had never seen such a pitiful scene before.

By August 17 all of Sicily was in Allied hands. Patton entered Messina following his faithful General Truscott, who reached the city very early in the morning. Patton came on a jeep around noon with photographers and newsreel operators who had been closely following every step he took since the invasion. He arrived ahead of Montgomery, winning the race against his British friend and rival to capture Sicily's last bastion. Patton found the town completely empty. The population had fled into the countryside to avoid the heavy bombing that had reduced many parts of the city to rubble. Over 100,000 German and Italian troops had managed to cross the Straits of Messina into Calabria, taking dozens of tanks, trucks, and artillery pieces, large and small, with them. The occupation of Sicily ranks among the greatest Allied operations of World War II, even though it failed in a sense because of the unusually high casualties, defective planning, and use of the complex military machinery set up at the Casablanca conference.

Yet both British and Americans were very well informed about conditions on that Mediterranean island.

The Intelligence Services

Long before any military planning involving the landing sites had started, the intelligence agencies of both countries had set up a meticulous espionage activity to gather a basic picture of the social, economic, and political situation existing on the island. The Allies therefore landed in possession of a vast wealth of information. A booklet filled with news, *Sicily Zone Handbook 1943,* bearing a Top Secret stamp of the British Foreign Office, was distributed to British officers a few months before D-Day and contained detailed information on the Sicilian population, its habits, traditions, and specifically the individuals who played a role in governing the island. Sicily's municipalities were listed alphabetically and each one included all kinds of data: from the name of the podestà (mayor) to that of the parish priest and the station master; whether there was a health official present; to information about banks, hospitals, and corporative organizations. An entire chapter discussed the role played by the Mafia, with details as to its origins, structure, the highlights of its traditional use of violence, the principles upon which the mafioso based his allegiance to the organization, such as "omertà," that was thought of as a quality setting him apart from existing social laws. The interest displayed by the British toward the Mafia's power in their little booklet should not be underestimated. In anticipation of the occupation of the island and setting up a military government that would have managed the political administration of the occupied territories, the intelligence services thought that they would have to deal with the Mafia and that military personnel about to land in Sicily should have at a minimum some kind of basic information.

The British had assembled a wealth of data on Italy through a vast web of informers that had been set up long before the American involvement. Italian spies provided a lot of intelligence that Churchill happily paid for long before Italy even entered the war. This was an endless engagement by men and women who were ready to be in the front lines along with the resistance fighters, happy to betray Mussolini's Fascist regime and die for the British cause.

American intelligence operated very differently since Sicily was actually a testing ground for the very new and imposing intelligence and counterintelligence apparatus the United States had set up during the Second World War. Information about Sicily was the sum of the efforts of the men in two important agencies: the Office of Strategic Services (OSS) and the Office of Naval Intelligence (ONI) that began approaching Italo-Americans in New York and other cities in the United States in 1941 and obtained up-to-date material on Sicily. These were mostly illustrated postcards, family pictures, school textbooks on history and geography and literature and private diaries. As we shall see later, this huge pool of information was made possible thanks to the work of naval intelligence following the agreement reached with Mafia boss Lucky Luciano, who had kept close ties to Sicily's Mafia leaders despite his long absence from the island and his last ten years in State prison.

The collection of information on Sicily was hugely successful for both American intelligence operations. The same cannot be said for operations in the field immediately following the landings, especially those undertaken by the OSS. Coordination problems and serious organizational mistakes surfaced in specific operations. When OSS agents arrived on the island to carry out what they had carefully trained for in the United States they had not only to deal with the problems of a land they didn't know but most of all with a military plan giving them far too much leeway for improvisation. On D-Day many OSS and ONI secret agents landed at Gela and elsewhere on the beaches along with Patton's troops, to pave the way for the army, but these "penetration squads," as they were called, of agents disguised as civilians who were sometimes guided by peasants eager to collaborate, often had to keep up with the speed of the American advance. At the end of the war an OSS agent recounted an episode confirming the absence of coordination. He was disguised as a peasant traveling on foot ahead of the U.S. Third Division under General Truscott's command in its race to Palermo. He was to keep the commander informed of the security on the road ahead. On a disrupted country road he suddenly noticed that he had been "overtaken" by Truscott's armored convoy. In disbelief he swallowed the dust kicked up by the vehicles and kept walking until he reached the nearest forward base where some soldiers were having their rations. He stood in line with his plate oblivious of the fact that he was dressed in civilian clothes. When he gave his plate to receive his rations someone kicked him so hard as to make him fall on the ground. Furious he answered with a whole list of dirty words and the other men then understood who he really was. To him, though, it was clear that there was something wrong with his orders. Those soldiers were not supposed to be there, at least not on that day or at that time.

American Intelligence

As the complex machinery of American intelligence services expanded very quickly, it went into new areas whose mission often remained unclear even to the men on the inside. Some organizations appeared for the specific purpose of providing support for military operations; others, such as the traditional intelligence service G2, were often no longer in sync with overall Allied strategy. The military leadership, while always wary of espionage and international intrigue, now viewed these as weapons that when put to good use could actually speed up the end of the war and save lives. This kind of activity was very risky politically but it captured the imagination of the American public and was high on the list of President Roosevelt's projects.

The need for an intelligence service made up of well-trained secret agents who were to be deployed in the battlefields of Europe and the Pacific was very much on Roosevelt's mind following the ignominious sinking of the U.S. Pacific fleet at Pearl Harbor on December 7, 1941. The day after the attack FDR was faced with a dilemma: how could the Japanese organize an offensive operation of that magnitude without American intelligence being aware of it? He found no immediate or easy answer to that question but he knew that it was no longer possible to continue operating as in peacetime and that U.S. internal security was suddenly placed at a very high risk. The Office of Strategic Services was therefore set up on June 13, 1942, with many internal departments to work with the Office of Naval Intelligence the Navy's intelligence arm; G-2, the Army's intelligence division and the Counter

Intelligence Corps (CIC) that handled counterespionage and had been created during the First World War.

President Harry Truman would dissolve the Office of Strategic Services in October 1945 and replace it with the Central Intelligence Group CIG, which would be renamed the CIA in September 1947. The Central Intelligence Agency is the key component among today's sixteen American intelligence services.

The Office of Strategic Services

The OSS was divided in various branches with a total of ten thousand full-time men and women. The most important sections were Secret Intelligence (SI), where secret information was collected, evaluated, and distributed; Special Operations (SO), in charge of making contact with overseas clandestine groups to create confusion within enemy ranks, engage in sabotage and finance guerrilla groups useful to American military objectives; Research and Analysis (R&A), which encompassed historical, economic, political, and social research (this branch was very active during the months that preceded the landings in Sicily in gathering detailed information on the island and its inhabitants); the Morale branch (MO) specialized in black propaganda; X-2 counterintelligence infiltrated agents into enemy armies. Each branch had tens of millions of dollars at its disposal without being required to account to Congress for the expenditure of these large amounts of money.

Roosevelt appointed General William J. Donovan, one of the most colorful figures of U.S. intelligence, to head the new agency. His daring and physical courage earned him the nickname of Wild Bill. FDR knew Donovan well and had already appointed him to head a new agency, Office of the Coordinator of Information (COI), on July 11, 1941. The COI actually became OSS in 1942.

Donovan had been one of the most decorated officers of the First World War and even after he returned to his activity as a Wall Street lawyer and a Republican party politician, he continued to serve the U.S. government. During the 1930s he traveled to Europe on his own initiative and happened to be in Spain in 1936; he had personally wit-

nessed Italy's invasion of Ethiopia and had been appointed ambassa-
dor-at-large by Roosevelt, in charge of monitoring political develop-
ments in Europe and the Middle East. After the Nazis occupied
Poland he was asked to go to London to assess Britain's defenses
against a possible German invasion and in the process established
strong ties to British intelligence. New technologies and the activities
of British intelligence were fascinating to Donovan, especially
RADAR, which he termed a "devilish" device allowing the operator to
spot incoming aircraft at a distance. The organizational innovations of
the British, and especially the techniques used to stop German agents
and turn them into double agents to fight a war that was becoming
increasingly brutal, had stimulated his curiosity. He also analyzed the
reorganization of British Foreign Intelligence (MI6), renamed Secret
Intelligence Service (SIS), as the structure that Donovan followed in
creating the new American intelligence service. He also studied the
new Special Operation Executive (SOE), created by Churchill in 1940,
whose agents were specifically trained to infiltrate those countries
occupied by the Nazis and help the various resistance movements
through sabotage aimed at damaging Germany's most important
weapons manufacturing plants.

Donovan was extremely rigid and inflexible in establishing the
guidelines for recruitment into the OSS. He needed reliable people
who spoke foreign languages and had traveled to foreign countries.
They had to be well educated but also thoroughly ruthless individuals
at the same time. Besides ambitious young men obsessed with
becoming secret agents, Donovan recruited men and women from
wealthy American society: bankers, millionaires, stockholders in large
companies, political leaders, and journalists. Wild Bill also used his
connections to the British secret services and their major contribution
would be the organization of a training camp called Camp X near
Ottawa in Canada, where new OSS recruits were given thorough
training by their British colleagues from SOE. Geoffrey Jones, a
veteran of Camp X, remembers:

> Just for fun we would often put together actual missions to test
> the FBI's efficiency. We pretended to blow up a navy yard in

Baltimore and we broke into a steel mill in Philadelphia. It was fun because we would always get away with it. The first time we left a piece of paper in the mill's furnace, the second time we made a phone call saying that there was a bomb in the mill. The FBI agents were not at all happy about this, naturally. If they caught us we had a phone number they should call to receive confirmation we really were regular OSS members and didn't want to blow up the steel mill. But sometimes they didn't place the call for two days, so it was best to avoid getting caught.

OSS was able to set up a branch office at 72 Grosvenor Street in London on condition that no American operations originate from the United Kingdom. Donovan would always abide by that request.

Secret Intelligence, Italian Section

On November 7, 1942, in Operation Torch (the occupation of French North Africa) the Allied invasion force landed in Morocco and Algeria. The OSS quickly opened a branch in Algiers under Henry Hyde to support secret agents who were to land in Sicily with General Patton's army.

In the winter of 1941, as planning for an invasion of Nazi occupied Europe from the Italian peninsula got underway, David K. Bruce, who at the time was the head of secret intelligence, decided to set up an Italian section headed by Earl Brennan of the State Department. War in the Mediterranean gave the OSS the opportunity to experiment with secret operations plans, from information gathering to special guerrilla actions, psychological warfare, and battlefield reconnaissance. Since Pearl Harbor, Bruce and Brennan had agreed on a detailed strategy to take action in Italy using their contacts with Crown Prince Umberto of Savoy to convince him that Italy would do best to exit the war as quickly as possible. No such action was undertaken, since Brennan found out that Prince Umberto "was not that strong in his opposition to Mussolini."

During the summer of 1942 the Italian section initiated a large program to contact Italian anti-Fascist organizations and Italo-American labor groups in New York. A nationwide recruiting effort began along with a training project for new agents at the OSS facilities. A plan of action for intelligence gathering was also put in place to cover the Mediterranean war zone, including preparation for the invasion of North Africa and Sicily that would be followed by that of the Italian mainland. These plans were drawn up with the help of Max Biagio Corvo, an army private (until his transfer to Algiers). He was originally a native of Sicily and was given the task of drafting a plan for espionage operations on the island. The Washington, D.C. staff of the Italian Section was enlarged in order to carry out the Corvo Plan, which also included a whole series of contacts with the most important spokesmen of anti-Fascist Italo-American groups that had emigrated to the United States. One of the first to be recruited was Dale MacAdoo, a cultured man who had studied in Italy and had returned to the U.S. after the declaration of war. MacAdoo spoke perfect Italian and had a strong passion for literature; he was therefore used as a library researcher for all kinds of information regarding Italy. During the recruitment phase, the Italian SI section provided support for Special Operations and the operational groups that were being set up. The commando operations were part of operational groups and their members were selected along ethnic lines. Joseph Bonfiglio, an NCO with a small staff of SI, worked hard at screening the linguistic capabilities of recruits who were being sent in by the army.

For the OSS to acquire complete freedom of action its officers cut off all ties to British intelligence, who at that time controlled the transportation lanes in the Mediterranean where no American interference was allowed. Since the beginning of the 1940s SIS had used its own agents in Italy, especially in the northeastern areas of the country: these were foreigners disguised as businessmen or tourists who brought back information. In 1942 the British used Italian spies to locate important military information, primarily photographs of war ships and harbors. Confirming that the British were already contemplating an attack on the southern coast of Italy, SIS had prepared a whole set of spying operations in southern Italy using some Italians who wound up in the hands of the Fascist police and the firing squad. This would be the fate of Antonio Gallo and Emilio Zappalà, two anti-Fascists who had joined British intelligence to set up a radio transmitter between Catania and Messina and organize a network of informants in Sicily to collect information on Axis weapons in the area. The two men landed at Pozzillo in October 1941, near Acireale, and after a few hours' march were stopped by the Carabinieri and handed over to Mussolini's counterespionage service. After a long trial Gallo and Zappalà were condemned to death and shot by firing squad in May 1943 at Forte Bravetta.

The recruitment of OSS agents in Europe was also extremely vigorous in 1942: at Bern, Switzerland, Allen Dulles was monitoring Nazi Germany while a vast espionage plan was being organized in Portugal, Spain, and North Africa. By November 1944 OSS agents and informers were a total of 13,000 men and women also operating in Burma, China, Thailand, and the Pacific as well.

Initial OSS Operations in Italy

In the spring of 1943 the Allied command asked Earl Brennan to prepare a team of operatives for the invasion of Sicily. The exact nature of the mission was not specified but agents in the Italian section were part of the G-2 section of Patton's Seventh Army under the name Experimental Detachment G-3, AFHQ. The unit's mission was to seize specific military codes and gather information for the upcoming Italian campaign. The Italian section had prepared a group of agents to land on the island in the first days of June but headquarters cancelled the operation at the last minute, fearing that any failure of the mission would alert coastal defenses about Operation Husky. On June 29, 1942, OSS Italian section sent its first group of agents into Sardinia. Five men, including a radio operator, landed on the northwestern coast of the island to gather intelligence on Italian units on the coast and assess their actual defensive capability. The group reached the island on a small boat but the turbulent waters forced them to land far from the chosen location and the next day the five were easily captured by Italian sentries. Other OSS agents were sent to Corsica, where a thick web of informers uncovered German and Italian battle plans in the event of an Allied landing. The clandestine radio operated by the OSS sent its first message back to Algeria on December 25, 1942, and continued with almost daily broadcasts until May 1943. But both Corsica and Sardinia were minor objectives for the Allies compared to Sicily, where they were to actually land a few months later.

In the course of 1942 information regarding the island reached Earl Brennan's desk uninterruptedly. It was all meticulous and careful work, the result of scores of the OSS personnel's involvement, but for the most part by Italo-Americans of all social classes who one way or another had some affinity to Sicily. They included anti-Fascist expatriates for political reasons as well as immigrant laborers, men of culture, businessmen, hardened criminals—the only requirement being that one had to be of Sicilian descent and have no living relatives on the island.

During the preparations of Operation Husky the involvement of well-known Mafia bosses such as Lucky Luciano became the exclusive area of ONI but inevitably that agreement would also involve other American military units operating on the island. These also included AMG or Allied Military Government officers who were to meet key members of Sicilian organized crime not just to obtain information regarding the island but, as we shall see later, to use their local power to further the struggle against the Communist party in Sicily.

Before we begin the investigation that will lead us to discovering the plans of the various American intelligence units, the names of agents who took part in the landings, and the OSS documents proving the connection between the Allies and organized crime for the invasion of Sicily, we must examine some key characters of the American and Sicilian Mafias who were prominent during those years.

Chapter 2

The American and Sicilian Mafias

Lucky Luciano and Calogero Vizzini

It was only in the 1950s that the American public would find out how from the beginning of the twentieth century a hidden element had developed and prospered within the social and economic fabric of American life. The revelation of the existence of organized crime to the extent that it had become a part of the national scene by infiltrating every vital sector of society, came as a complete surprise.

In 1950 Senator Estes Kefauver, a Tennessee Democrat, led a committee investigating criminal activity over state lines by gangsters in America and alerted public opinion while creating a panic inside the criminal organizations. In the previous decade political corruption and rising crime had developed all too easily in the United States and the American people's craving for decency and honesty became embodied in the senator who had the courage to bring dozens of Mafia bosses in front of the court of public opinion, including corrupt politicians, bankers, and other Italo-American underworld-related figures. Kefauver was 47 when he decided to blow the whistle on organized crime in America. From May 10, 1950 to May 1, 1951, he was the chairman of the Special Committee to Investigate Crime in Interstate Commerce, better known as the Kefauver Committee in the U.S. Senate. He used the new medium of television that was just beginning to grow into a mammoth industry; it allowed him to enter America's living rooms, feeding the public's demand for honesty and justice. The six-foot, bespectacled senator with the pleasant, honest face offered some simple truisms and did so in public: "There are many criminals in America....," he said.

Kefauver took innumerable statements in the twelve months the committee was active and managed to force many gangsters to talk. Hundreds of underworld figures received subpoenas and many of them were frantic at the idea of appearing in public in front of photographers and journalists. Never before had so many shady individuals appeared in front of a commission of inquiry: Mafiosi, intermediaries, murderers, drivers, burglars, blackmailers, prostitutes, wives, and lovers of top crime bosses. Many of the gangsters' right-hand men disappeared rather than take the witness stand and some even fled the country.

Kefauver traveled some fifty thousand miles around the United States during the hearings. Using radio and television (newsmen were constantly asking him to make statements and when he was on the air ratings would jump to thirty million viewers and listeners) he became so famous in a few months that he received literally tons of letters, up to sixty thousand, plus thousands of telegrams. America was enthusiastic about the senator's inquiry because it revealed the underside of a vast political and criminal conspiracy in the United States. One letter even stated, "I'm a little gangster. I don't know anything but I'm sure you are a very sharp guy."

It was not easy to extract information from such a large number of underworld figures. The recurring and mostly arrogant answer was the pleading of the Fifth Amendment: "I refuse to answer on the grounds that it may incriminate me." It was easy to detect through the eyes and body language of the gangsters on the stand some kind of defiance but then many caved, in especially once President Truman allowed the committee to gain access to the income tax returns of politicians who were testifying. The first hearing took place in Miami on May 26, 1950. Other hearings followed in New Orleans, Kansas City, Detroit, Washington, D.C., Chicago, New York, Las Vegas, Philadelphia, San Francisco, Los Angeles, St. Louis, Cleveland, and Tampa. After hearing hundreds of witnesses and reading thousands of pages of testimony, Kefauver concluded that "an underworld syndicate with ramifications around the country" existed in the United States, whose activities were controlled by "a corrupt and cynical association of gangsters, corrupt politicians and businessmen and lawmen without a conscience, hiding behind a mask of respectability." Kefauver called this a mysterious and furtive world that was difficult to understand.

During Prohibition the gangs ordinarily engaged in murder and violence. Over the years the gangsters reached an understanding: they became more cautious and agreed to split the territories. The bosses began dressing well, improving themselves, and using lawyers and tax experts. The image of the uncouth Al Capone changed to the business-man-like Frank Costello, the most influential leader in the American underworld.

Once it was all put together, a relatively small group of men, led by Lucky Luciano, had forged an illegal empire rivaling any legitimate one.

I'll bet in the days when me and my guys got our whiskey business together, we had a bigger company than Henry Ford. We controlled plants, warehouses, and all kinds of manufacturing; we had a fantastic shipping business; and our drivers had to drive good and shoot straight. We had bookkeepers that Lansky used to watch over like a hawk, and these wasn't little guys with green eyeshades. These guys—and we even had plenty of girls as bookkeepers—were guys with photographic memories because not too much of their numbers ever got on paper. We had exporters and importers, all kinds of help that any corporation needs, only we had more. And we had lawyers by the carload, and they was on call twenty-four hours a day. Guys always told me later that I should've put my brains to runnin' a legit business and I'd have been a tremendous success. But I wouldn't've enjoyed it like what I was doin'.

Chicago and New York were the centers of the underworld: the "Capone Syndicate" still used the name of its late founder, now deceased; then the various factions run by Frank Costello, Joe Adonis, and Meyer Lansky. Their ties were based upon personal agreements and a "reciprocal tolerance among leaders more than on rules and regulations." Formal meetings were unnecessary and they could take place anywhere.

The question asked by the committee at the very first hearing was: who was behind the local gangs that together made up the national organized crime syndicate? The investigation provided a clear and unambiguous answer: the Mafia was operating behind the gangsters, an international criminal organization that had its roots in Sicily. The Mafia was able to corrupt everyone, even policemen and investigators who pocketed tens of thousands of dollars to protect the gangsters. There were also sheriffs and state governors, who were financing their election campaigns with the percentages they received from the criminal enterprises they were protecting.

They had plenty to offer the politicians who helped them, those candidates for the public's vote and trust. They had the money to finance any campaign, to make any tractable politician a wealthy man; they had the contacts and the knowledge to turn a willing politician on to lucrative deals in road-building, construction and more—the list is endless—and they had the strong-arm forces to terrorize any of their candidates' opponents and to incline voters to cast their ballots the "right way.[1]

None of the activities of Lucania—bootlegging, gambling, loan sharking, garment center invasions—could have succeeded without the protection of the city's political and police structure. The price was high, but to him and his partners, it was worth the cost.

---

1. Martin Gosch and Richard Hammer, *The Last Testament of Lucky Luciano* (London: Macmillan, 1974). Hereafter, Gosch and Hammer.

… I personally helped elect more than eighty guys over a short time, all votin' my way, aldermen, councilmen, mayors, congressmen, even senators. They was mine. I picked 'em. I elected 'em. They belonged to me, lock, stock, and barrel.[2]

The picture of America provided by the Kefauver committee made ordinary people shudder. The surprise was even greater for a citizenry accustomed to viewing the government and its members as being morally superior; the public then became incredulous as some of the reasons for this state of affairs became known. Federal agencies bore much of the responsibility, the IRS especially because it had not dig deeply enough into the kind of income tax evasion that was practiced by most well-known Mafia bosses. The FBI was also to blame when it protected the secrecy of its sources of information. Mobsters had infiltrated over seventy different kinds of legitimate businesses, often eliminating the original entrepreneurs.

For the first time Kefauver provided a realistic and up-to-date definition of the Mafia. Until then it had been a faceless, almost abstract entity in the mind of the American people. There were frightening memories of the Black Hand, which had been responsible in the early part of the century for a whole series of homicides tied to extortions. The public knew about the investigations by Joe Petrosino, the famous Italo-American detective, and his murder by Vito Cascio Ferro on March 12, 1909, in the Piazza della Marina in Palermo. Don Vito was acquitted of the charge of murder because a member of parliament, De Michele Ferrantelli, gave testimony that they had spent several days together at some distance from Palermo.

Don Vito Cascio Ferro was the epitome of the "man of respect": tall, handsome, and sporting a reddish beard, he would settle any dispute among the population of his village. He was 39 when he arrived in New York from Bisacquino in 1901, following the strange case of the kidnapping of nineteen-year-old Baroness Clorinda Peritelli di Valpetroso, in which he was implicated. The young woman had been kidnapped by three bandits in Palermo, taken to a country house where she spent the night under the watchful eyes of a woman. She

---

2. Ibid.

was freed the next morning, probably after her family agreed to pay a heavy ransom. The perpetrators were quickly identified and the young baroness recognized Vito Cascio Ferro as one of them, as well as Girolamo Campisi, a student who had no prior arrest record. Cascio Ferro told the Carabinieri that the young Campisi had fallen in love with the girl and asked him to fulfill his dream. Everyone in the village believed him despite the fact that the beautiful Clorinda denied having any love interest for the handsome Girolamo. Cascio Ferro was therefore condemned to three years in prison with the sentence being forgiven almost immediately. But Don Vito did not stay in America very long; he returned to Sicily in 1904. During those three years he managed to reorganize a number of gangs that were engaging in petty crime. He had started the protection racket by giving his young recruits the following orders: "Become the paternal protectors of every shop-keeper in New York." A murder investigation put Cascio Ferro on the path of Joe Petrosino. To avoid going to prison Ferro quickly left New York but was so unhappy about it that he slipped a newspaper clipping with the detective's picture in his pocket, hoping to be able to kill him himself some day.

The Mafia described by the Kefauver committee was very different from that of the early 1900s. "It's not a fairy tale they read to children in Sicily. It has scarred the face of America with all kinds of crimes and it has an international leader. His name is Lucky Luciano."

Lucky Luciano, the godfather of the godfathers, the "capo di tutti i capi," in a bigoted and racist America had paradoxically turned into a "hero of the underworld" after bringing the Mafia up to date and becoming its number one leader. He was able to hold on to his leader-ship position up to the time of his death at age 64 on January 26, 1962, at Capodichino Airport in Naples as he was expecting the arrival of a producer who wanted to finance a film about his life. *Time* magazine named Lucky Luciano one of the "One hundred important people of the twentieth century," along with Walt Disney, Henry Ford, and Bill Gates. The article described Luciano as the "criminal orchestrator," the one who "reinvented and modernized the Mafia by managing it as a national business that concentrates on truly important matters and views violence as an impediment to business. It has managed to have an influence in America from Broadway to every area of public order, from national politics to the world economy."[3]

Even after Prohibition was dumped, I was runnin' one of the biggest businesses in the world. We was in a hundred different things, legit and illegit. If you add it all up, we—I mean, the guys all over the country—we was doin' a business that was grossin' maybe a couple billion dollars a year. I was like the head of that big company, not the Boss of Bosses, but as a guy a lot of people came to for advice, a guy everybody expected to be in on the big decisions. But there was no way I could know what was goin' on everywhere all the time.[4]

Kefauver also handled the embarrassing issue of the relationship between the Mafia boss and U.S. intelligence during World War II. The senator wrote in one of his reports:

During the Second World War there were many rumors about some valuable services performed by Luciano, who was in jail at the time, for the military with respect to the planned invasion of his native Sicily. When we investigated we found some rather contradictory versions.

Kefauver wanted to call the man who had freed Lucky Luciano from state prison as a witness, but former New York governor Thomas Dewey did not appear. However, George White, an agent with the Federal Bureau of Narcotics, shed some light on various aspects of the issue:

During an investigation undertaken by my office I was approached by a man called August Del Grazio, on Luciano's behalf, who was a drug smuggler who said he was sent by two lawyers and by Frank Costello. He said Luciano had many powerful connections to the Italian underworld and was one of the top

---

3. *Time* magazine.
4. Gosch and Hammer.

leaders of the Mafia. He would be willing to use his position in the Mafia to pave the way for U.S. secret agents, thus making Sicily a much easier target. In exchange the military authorities would set Luciano free on parole, allowing him to go to Sicily and prepare everything.

The Kefauver investigation left many questions unanswered about the relationship between U.S. intelligence and the Mafia leaders and it was only later on, with the investigation headed by District Attorney William B. Herlands, that some of its more worrisome aspects that could embarrass the U.S. Navy were revealed. We shall discuss Operation Underworld, the code name for the collaboration between Mafia and Naval intelligence, later on.

The man who headed the Cosa Nostra and his ascent to the pinnacle of American organized crime, namely Salvatore Lucania, *aka* Lucky Luciano, is the key element to this incredible story.

Salvatore was barely ten when in April 1907 the Lucania family left the village of Lercara Friddi near Palermo to immigrate to America. They found a small apartment near Fourteenth Street in Manhattan, which was then teeming with Sicilians and Neapolitans, but also Jews and Irish who had arrived earlier in the larger wave of immigration at the turn of the century. Lucky was born on November 11, 1897, after Giuseppe and Concetta but before Bartolo and Francesca. Antonio, his father, was a hard working honest laborer who quickly became an American citizen. According to U.S. immigration law both Salvatore and his mother Rosalia Capporelli and the other brothers and sisters also became American citizens. It was therefore natural to also Americanize their names so they became Joseph, Connie, Fannie, Bart, and Salvatore was changed to Sal. But he did not like the name and thought that Sal sounded too much like a girl's first name, but he went along with it in order to not displease his mother. He decided to change his name in prison some years later when he was sentenced for smuggling narcotics. The police had discovered that he was carrying two ounces of heroin carefully concealed in the headband of his hat, like the ones manufactured by his employer, the Goodman Hat Company. On Christmas morning in 1916 the doors of New York's

Hampton Farms Penitentiary opened and Sal at 19 decided to go by the name of Charles or Charlie. Salvatore Lucania disappeared on that day.

Charlie grew up among gangs of juvenile delinquents, offering protection to the Jews and more vulnerable kids in exchange for money:

> My old man kept sayin' the neighborhood was getting' worse, that there was gangs of young guys around my age who was knockin' off stores, grabbin' handbags from old ladies, stuff like that. He said every kid in the neighborhood was growin' up to be a crook.[5]

He began learning how to handle himself as a street hood but his true Mafia education came when he became a soldier in the crime family headed by Joe Masseria, also known as Joe the "Boss." Masseria was a round tub of lard without a neck who spent his days in a huge leather armchair and couldn't even stand up following the enormous amounts of food he usually ingested. Charlie, along with other young criminals like Vito Genovese, Frank Costello, and Albert Anastasia, was in charge of delivering and receiving drugs and liquor while keeping the other part of the empire built on prostitution, gambling, and illegal bets under control. The First World War had just begun and these young hoods were in their twenties. Frank Costello was originally from Cosenza in Calabria and spoke in a perpetually gravelly low voice. His real name was Francesco Castiglia and his refined manners hid a cruel and ruthless disposition. He was a master at underhanded subterfuge and managed very well in the financial and banking world. Vito Genovese was an ambitious young gangster in Manhattan's Little Italy. He was short and stocky with a broad face and without any hesitation more than ready to kill anyone who got in his way. Albert Anastasia was also ruthless and extremely violent as a key player in the longshoremen's union: murder to him was a way of life.

It was during this time that Charlie met Meyer Lansky, a Russian Jew who came to the New York ghetto in the Lower East Side at age nine and whose mathematical and business acumen quickly promoted

---

5. Ibid.

him into the gang's chief accountant. In spite of being very small and skinny he never let anyone intimidate him. His friends thought of him as a genius and he even created a theory of organized crime known as "Lansky's Law": "If you have large quantities of what the public wants but can't get then you can satisfy the demand and collect the dough."

Prohibition provided the perfect illustration of this "rule." A new member quickly joined the gang, Benjamin "Benny" Siegel, also nick-named "Bugsy," an elegantly dressed dandy who loved sports cars and would eventually borrow several million dollars to build the gambler's paradise of Las Vegas, the mecca he masterminded in the Nevada desert.

Charlie Lucania was an amiable and friendly fellow, always ready and willing to help and listen. Although naturally prone to violence he also wanted to please and was ready to engage in the worst kind of criminal activity as long as he could live like a rich man in the greatest luxury while earning the respect of his peers. As he remembered many years later: "Looking north of Fourteenth Street, into the kingdom of wealth, I began to realize how people were living and the things they had. I would dream that one day that territory would all be mine, that I'd tame it and walk those streets like a king in his kingdom."

He knew that if he went to the top he would have to take much greater risks. The Prohibition Era, with its ban on all alcoholic beverages in bars, became the vehicle that enabled Lucky Luciano and many others to break into big business. Charlie had found a theory that together with that of his friend Meyer Lansky proved to be un-assailable: "Every man is a thief, only most people don't have the guts to steal. That's the big difference between us and the guys who say they're honest. We have the guts to do what they'd like to do but frightens them too much."

For many years Big Jim Colosimo controlled the territory in Chicago where he had made a fortune in prostitution, gambling, and running Colosimo's Café, a nightspot patronized by the city's wealthy citizens and where on a few occasions Enrico Caruso came to sing. Colosimo was a well-respected boss until the day he found it necessary to seek the help of Johnny Torrio, an up and coming murderer who came from Naples and was nicknamed "Johnny The Terrible." The

Black Hand had a contract out on Big Jim but Torrio managed to help him out of his troubles. Colosimo paid Torrio by giving him a whorehouse fully equipped with a dozen beautiful women, a rich nineteenth century décor, and a long list of clients. Torrio thanked Colosimo but suggested they go into bootlegging because the new laws of prohibition had made brothels a less lucrative business. The old boss preferred to stay with what he knew best and his hundreds of beautiful women and the thousands of Johns scattered all over America. Torrio got mad and summoned to Chicago a young killer from New York named Alfonso "Al" Capone. A few months later, on May 11, 1920, Big Jim Colosimo was shot to death in one of his restaurants. Torrio and Al Capone, also known as "Scarface Al" because of a deep scar across his face, became partners in the illegal liquor rackets.

Johnny Torrio was the brains and Capone provided the necessary hard muscle. Once Johnny became the target of a few bitter godfathers who had been cut off from the big money liquor business Al Capone suddenly found himself alone in charge of a Chicago that was increasingly corrupt and steeped in vice. On February 14, 1929, St. Valentine's Day, Capone consolidated his power by having seven leaders of Bugs Moran's gang shot to death in a garage as a signal to their boss, who was refusing to pay tribute. Every newspaper in America printed stories about the massacre and Capone, calling the short fat man with a huge cigar constantly stuck in his mouth and who lived in luxury at the Lexington Hotel "public enemy number one."

One evening in a New York restaurant Al Capone was sampling some of the best Italian wines in the company of Charlie Lucania and a few other associates of his. At the end of the meal Capone lifted his glass and looked at the young Lucania straight in the eyes said: "To my cousin Charlie, who will be New York's liquor king." In his mind Charlie had already worked out the way he was going to fulfill his growing ambitions. The gang continued to grow with the arrival of another handsome young Neapolitan, Giuseppe Antonio Doto, who at age 18 was already a professional thief and was using the assumed name of Joseph A. Adonis.

In 1923, at age twenty-six, Charlie Lucania was ready to make his big move. He was still working for Joe Masseria, whose power was being threatened in the mid 1920s by Salvatore Maranzano, a boss sent to America by Don Vito Cascio Ferro to straighten out matters among Sicilian-American gangs in New York. Maranzano tried to talk Charlie into betraying Masseria and ordered that he be beaten when he refused to do so. On October 16, 1929, Charlie was bleeding and near death in a Staten Island warehouse, his mouth sealed shut with masking tape. He had managed to drag himself to Highland Boulevard. He was given the nickname "Lucky" because he survived the brutal beating at the hands of Maranzano's men. He added the nickname to the new one he had picked: Luciano. From then on at age thirty-two he became Lucky Luciano and his recent experience meant that New York was ready for a major bloody war.

The Wall Street Crash of October 29, 1929, was the beginning of a panic in the United States that would decimate entire fortunes and force many people into poverty and financial difficulties. The bootleg liquor market was also affected, as well as gambling and prostitution. Vito Genovese wasted no time in exploiting narcotics as a new venture, but Luciano was not convinced. The white powder was just a source of problems.

Vito Genovese had another plan to provide the public with ways to escape daily reality. Despite Luciano's admonitions, he had not ceased dealing in narcotics. Now he wanted to expand. The profits, he said, were so much greater than anything else and once a sale was made, the customer was hooked and he had to keep coming back for more. Luciano was just as convinced that narcotics led only to trouble; he knew that from his own experience. "I kept tryin' to argue Vito out of it, but he wouldn't listen. Maybe I should've thrown him out, but you can't just throw a guy like that out cold. Especially not after all the things Vito done for me." .... So he told Genovese,

I don't wanna know nothin' about it. If you wanna do it, do it; anybody you wanna do it with, do it with. But don't tell me about it. I don't want it and I don't wanna know about it. Just remember,

Vito, if you get in trouble with that stuff, you'll have to bail yourself out.[6]

Luciano would not accept dealing in drugs on his territory, at least at that time, and instead turned to a new business borne of the Depression: shylocking. At the same time, however, he continued to manage brothels and distribute slot machines, a business that was beginning to flourish in the early 1930s.

If Luciano had definitely ruled out narcotics, he was very much in favor of (and on a much bigger level than ever) the old scheme called usury. The regular bankers were extremely skittish about lending what little money they had, and potential borrowers were forced to look elsewhere. That meant the underworld, which had amassed millions of dollars in cash during Prohibition—for it only engaged in cash businesses. Within a year after the crash, so fast did their shylocking business grow, millions of dollars had been put on the street in the form of usurious loans. With companies failing at a disastrous rate, it became senseless to wreak physical violence on the defaulting borrower. So more and more companies in the garment business, meat packing, milk, trucking, and other industries vital to the city's economic life began to fall under mob control, and were increasingly used as legitimate fronts for innumerable other illicit activities.

Loan sharking took advantage of the need to borrow; gambling in its various forms played to the dream of a windfall. The numbers racket suddenly surged way beyond the expectations of Luciano, Lansky, Costello, and the others; Costello's slots, after a letdown, began to regurgitate a never-ending stream of nickels, dimes, and quarters. Betting on everything and anything seemed to be the passion of those who had nothing but hope that a bet would maybe pay off.[7]

A Mafia summit was convened in May of the same year in Atlantic City, attended by the major Mafia leaders in the United States with the New York delegation being led by Lucky Luciano. The old bosses, Masseria and Maranzano, were gone and Luciano used the meeting to point out the need to "refresh" the methods used by criminal organiza-

---

6. Ibid.
7. Ibid.

tions in managing a vast illegal empire. It was no longer to be one gang under the rule of a single leader but rather "a group of organizations acting in concert according to decisions reached at the top by men of equal importance." Everyone liked the idea and by the end of the meeting Luciano had become one of the most important heads of the American underworld.

The relationship between Masseria and Maranzano was by now beyond repair. Lucky Luciano understood that the time to replace them was at hand. He intimated to Maranzano that he was his ally and promised to have Masseria killed. It was a promise he firmly intended to keep and on April 15, 1931, Vito Genovese, Joe Adonis, Albert Anastasia, and Bugsy Siegel burst into the Nuova Villa Tammaro restaurant at Coney Island and fired twenty-five rounds into Joe "The Boss." Luciano had drawn Masseria into that trap in the restaurant under the guise of deciding how to eliminate Maranzano. Masseria was having spaghetti with clam sauce and was playing cards.

Luciano and Masseria were the last patrons. Luciano suggested that they relax for a while and play a game of Klob, a Russian-Hungarian two-handed card game that Masseria had learned from Frank Costello. Masseria hesitated for a moment, then agreed to a short game, reminding Luciano that there was still work to be done back at head-quarters.[8]

They had played one hand, and had just dealt the cards for a second, when Luciano got up from the table and told Masseria he had to go to the men's room. Masseria relaxed, enjoying a second bottle of wine.

As soon as the lavatory door closed behind Luciano, the front door of the Villa Tammaro opened. The car that Luciano had driven from Manhattan had been followed at a discreet distance by a black limousine, driven by Ciro Terranova and carrying Vito Genovese, Joe Adonis, Albert Anastasia, and Bugsy Siegel. Those four burst into the restaurant, pulled out pistols, and began firing at Joe the Boss. More than twenty shots ricocheted around the room, six smashing directly into Masseria, who slumped over the table, face down, his blood

---

8. Ibid.

staining the white tablecloth; in his right hand dangled the ace of diamonds.[9]

And Luciano? He calmly emerged from the lavatory, took a look at the dead Masseria, called the police, and waited for them to arrive.

When the cops come, naturally they wanted to know whether I seen what happened. I said no, I didn't, and I didn't have no idea why somebody would want to kill Joe. They asked me where I was when it happened—and every newspaper printed that I said, "As soon as I finished dryin' my hands, I walked out to see what it was all about." That's an absolute lie. I said to them, "I was in the can takin' a leak. I always take a long leak." [10]

The old ways and the old leaders were finally dead and Charlie Lucky Luciano was king at last. The fallen ruler, Salvatore Maranzano, was given a send-off befitting his status—Luciano insisted on that— with the ritual long line of black limousines, flowers, tears and eulogies. Once Maranzano was laid to rest, Luciano announced that the old Don's autocratic ideas had been buried with him. The day of the absolute monarchy was over; henceforth there would be a constitutional government with respect for the rights of each group. Luciano was determined to neither alienate nor antagonize anyone; all should and would be treated as equals and allies.[11]

Maranzano was ecstatic and proclaimed himself top boss of the New York Mafia. He never thought that Luciano was already thinking of seeking revenge for the beating he had received a few years before. Lucky Luciano had decided to eliminate Maranzano and the old Mafia that prevented the rise of new businesses more attuned to the times. Those "Mustache Petes," as Luciano called them, had become intolerable.

Maranzano had it all now; he didn't waste a single day in startin' to make plans. He was gonna have the damnedest "inauguration"

---

9. Ibid.
10. Ibid.
11. Ibid.

that ever took place in the United States of America. In a few weeks after Masseria stopped bein' a pig and become a corpse, all Maranzano could think about was the day he was gonna be crowned king.[12]

But Luciano was just as determined that the reign would be brief. As Maranzano was planning his coronation, Luciano called together his own cabinet to put in motion the program that would place Charlie Lucky Luciano at the top of organized crime. The decision then was to move slowly, with patience, to let Maranzano initially proceed unopposed; they were sure Maranzano would help in bringing about his own downfall.

With almost naïve arrogance, Maranzano assumed that no one would dare challenge him, that any threats could be eliminated, with little difficulty. He sent out invitations to a formal crowning, to a ceremony of obeisance—more a command than an invitation—to hundreds of mob leaders and followers in New York and around the country. More than five hundred jammed a large banquet hall on the Grand Concourse in the Bronx, filling every chair in a prearranged order according to rank. On the dais, facing the throng, sat Maranzano on a large throne-like chair, rented from a theatrical prop warehouse specially for the occasion. On either side of him, he placed those he was about to install as his princes and lords, the heads of the various gangs and units. Luciano sat at his right hand, the designated crown prince.

The whole joint was practically covered with crosses, religious pictures, statues of the Virgin and saints I never heard of. Maranzano was the biggest cross nut in the world—he wore a cross around his neck, he had 'em stuffed in his pockets, wherever he was there was crosses all over the place. He was an absolute maniac on religion. In fact, he used to call guys in and bawl the shit out of 'em for not goin' to church. I remember one time—it was a little later—when Mike Miranda told me that Maranzano give it to him about the church and Mike said to him, "How can I go to

12. Ibid.

church when I just knocked off a guy?" He said Maranzano told him, "That has nothing to do with it. Religion is only concerned with a man's soul."[13]

When Maranzano rose, there was absolute silence. He spoke in Italian, often lapsing into Sicilian dialect and larding his speech with Latin quotations. He explained that a new day was dawning. There had been attempts, he said, from Chicago to thwart this meeting—there had been opposition to his endeavors to bring order, leadership, and discipline to the chaos and warring of recent years. All this he regretted, but the massing of all his good friends showed that such efforts have come to nothing.

Maranzano used every trick of an accomplished orator as he spoke, intoning, lowering his voice almost to a whisper to make his audience lean forward to catch his words, stretching out his arms in the attitude of benediction. Raising a clenched fist, he proclaimed himself the Supreme Ruler, the Boss of all Bosses—Capo di Tutti i Capi. He explained that no longer would he rule a separate organization of his own; everything would now be combined into a single organization under one rule—his. He would control a share of everything to be reaped by all the new "families" (a euphemism he ordered to replace the pejorative "gang" or "mob"), and he would later tell all the sub-leaders how large a share would be.[14]

Five months after Masseria's death during the so-called "Night of the Sicilian Vespers," Maranzano was killed by six Jewish gangsters masquerading as federal agents whom Luciano had personally trained. It was September 10, 1931, and all of Maranzano's closest men were killed with their boss. The massacre ended the contest to control the old Sicilian families. The police found a piece of paper in Maranzano's coat with a list of names of those he wanted to see dead: Luciano, Genovese, Costello, Adonis, and others. But Luciano had played his cards faster and won.

During those bloody years the FBI investigated but never used the word "Mafia" in any of its reports. J. Edgar Hoover was convinced

---

13. Ibid.
14. Ibid.

that even the killing of honest businessmen and merchants was part of the retribution among small gangs of criminals and therefore he never ordered the Bureau to go after organized crime specifically. The nation's top policeman had been blackmailed by the Mafia through some incriminating photographs with his assistant, Clyde Tolson. British journalist Anthony Summers has told the story of Hoover and the Mafia, revealing how he was in contact with several Mafia bosses, from Frank Costello to Meyer Lansky, and that homosexuality was his Achilles' heel. There is also a statement by Susan Rosenstiel, who was known for telling all kinds of stories, and who claimed to have seen none other than J. Edgar Hoover at a party dressed in women's clothes, silk stockings, black wig, and false eyelashes. A few incriminating photos of Hoover and Tolson landed in the hands of Meyer Lansky, who blackmailed the head of the FBI all his life.

The Birth of Cosa Nostra

The death of old Don Totò Maranzano also meant the end of the autocratic and centralized way of running the Mafia. Luciano wanted to rule by consensus and not through intimidation, as he told his closest collaborators.

Luciano announced that the old Don's autocratic ideas had been buried with him. The day of the absolute monarchy was over; henceforth there would be a "constitutional government" with respect for the rights of each group. Luciano was determined neither to alienate nor antagonize anyone; all should and would be treated as equals and allies.

From his experiences of the past decade, Luciano knew that he could remain at the top only if he eschewed fear and intimidation; he could not, as Masseria and Maranzano had tried to do, force into submission men such as Profaci, Bonanno, Mangano, Scalise, Gagliano, Capone, and the rest of his friends who had supported him and who gave him the respect that they wanted in return. He sensed, then, that if he rejected the offered throne in name, he would in fact soon receive it by force of circumstances. This was the Sicilian-Italian paradox that he understood—the yearning for leadership but the rejection of the autocratic leader.[15]

The business side of the Mafia had to move ahead, as Luciano repeated, and make progress and just like any other economic activity it had to find its own "legal space" within society. It had to carve out a permanent slot for itself within the life of the country certainly not in conflict with other powers of the State and especially not with law enforcement agencies, with whom all clashes and confrontations were to be avoided. Luciano's decision was based on three important choices: to reduce the hostility among criminal organizations through agreements on territories; to avoid confrontations with any government agency and whenever possible work with them to uncover any criminals; to guarantee that the Sicilian-American Mafia would have the dominant position among all other criminal associations by developing ties with politicians and influence over labor unions and the way Italian-Americans would vote in elections.

Meyer Lansky suggested that this organization be called the "Sicilian Union." Luciano, however, after working hard to Americanize the structure, still never wanted to call it a "union" but rather a Cosa Nostra ("Our thing") like any business and that it didn't belong to any single boss. It was a true criminal empire with money stashed away all over the world and business interests tied to many different commercial enterprises: an extraterritorial holding in the hands of a very small commission dominated by an oligarchy of leaders who were almost invariably of Sicilian origin and who would always follow Luciano's decisions.

Once he became the crowned boss of the new modern criminal organization and while repeating that he didn't feel he should be the sole leader, Luciano went through a few quiet years, spending most of his days relaxing in his luxurious apartment in the Waldorf Towers on Park Avenue, leased under the alias of Charles Ross, and his nights in New York's luxury nightclubs as the city slowly began reviving from the Crash of 1929 and the Great Depression.

---

15. Ibid.

Lucky Luciano is Arrested

In 1934 Attorney General Thomas E. Dewey of New York began a series of investigations into organized crime, concentrating on the extortion and prostitution rackets. On April 4, 1936, Dewey issued a warrant for the arrest of Lucky Luciano, who was being accused of running brothels and using the services of dozens of young women. The witnesses Dewey produced at the trial "were convincing and backed up the illegal vice charges." At his trial Luciano rejected the indictment and didn't think the prostitution charges would be taken seriously. He felt that even if he were found guilty he would receive a very light sentence. However, in his powerful summation Dewey was able to turn the evidence into an all-out attack on the rackets boss.

Outside the courtroom, Luciano was all smiles. He told reporters,

> I certainly expect to be acquitted. I don't know any of the people who took the stand and said they knew me or talked to me or overheard me in conversations. I never met any of them. I never was engaged in this racket at all. I never in my life met any of the codefendants, except Betillo, before this trial.

Then it was time for Dewey to have the final say. Admitting that many of his key witnesses were ordinary prostitutes, he told the jury it

> could not hold that a prostitute is unworthy of belief. You must give her story the same weight as you would to that of a respectable person. If you believe what she says, then the story stands and the fact that she is a prostitute is of no moment.

Coming to the end, he looked directly at the Boss. With rage he pointed at Luciano, who, he said, showed "a shocking, disgusting display of sanctimonious perjury—at the end of which I am sure not one of you had a doubt that before you is not a gambler, not a book-maker, but the greatest gangster in America." For seven hours Dewey had managed to transfix the jury.[16]

---

16. Ibid.

The jury found Luciano guilty on sixty-two counts relating to abetting prostitution and Judge Phillip J. McCook imposed a very heavy sentence on the thirty-eight year old Mafia boss: he was to spend from thirty to fifty years in jail. The prisoner was taken to Sing Sing state prison a few hours later where Dr. L. E. Kienholz, a deputy head psychiatrist at the prison clinic, wrote in a report that Luciano was a man "of extraordinary intelligence" but that there were "few chances he would be rehabilitated" because he was a "dangerous individual who should not be given too much freedom since he was a drug addict." Luciano was quickly transferred to the more secure prison at Dannemora, located in upstate New York.

After the sentencing Dewey made a number of statements to the press that drove The Boss crazy. "This," said Dewey, "was not a vice trial. It was a trial of the rackets…"

More than seeking revenge Luciano began searching for a way to get out of jail. He couldn't bear the thought of spending his life locked up in a cell but all he could do was to stay on his best behavior. Then with Pearl Harbor on December 7, 1941, America entered the war and that was his good fortune. It had been six years since Luciano had entered prison on June 18, 1936.

Don Calogero Vizzini

While Lucky Luciano had successfully modernized the Mafia, effecting the switch from the old logic of a single leader wielding absolute power, to the creation of a real crime syndicate with a board of directors heading Cosa Nostra, the Mafia in Sicily was identified with one man who had been running it very efficiently for decades: Don Calogero Vizzini, the Godfather of Villalba, a small town with houses made out of tuff in the hills of the vast lands of Miccichè, located in the middle of the province of Caltanissetta, known as Vallone. Himself a semi-illiterate (he had only attended elementary school with meager results), at a very young age Don Calò became the lieutenant of the bandit Vassallone, who had taught him that if he wanted something it was better to use words rather than weapons to obtain it. He toned down his brutal ways thanks to his uncle, who was a bishop, and his two brothers Giovanni and Salvatore, both of them priests who were much more interested in the pleasures of this world than in the promise of a better life after death and who remained close to Don Calò as he pursued his successful social and economic climb.

Born July 24, 1877, Calogero Vizzini belongs to a part of the history of Sicily characterized by the massive occupation of the land through the mobilization of large numbers of peasants, mostly veterans who were driven by socialists and by new political forces, like Father Luigi Sturzo's in the Partito Popolare (the precursor of the Christian Democrats).

This great popular movement reacting against one of the scourges of Sicily's economy, represented by vast landholdings (latifundia) concentrated in the hands of a few owners, created a split among the various criminal organizations, thus encouraging the rise of a new criminal group intent on benefiting from the peasant classes to climb up in society. Alongside the Mafia of the large landowners and lease holders, whose function it was to protect the profits of the estates, a lower middle class Mafia also emerged among the rural bourgeoisie. This Mafia was active using the cooperatives and the peasant leagues as the main vehicle for its own enrichment.

Calogero Vizzini managed to play both roles as old and new Mafioso. He was the friendly and highly respected Don Calò, known to the rich landowners of the Vallone, a man given a lavish welcome by the Princes of Trabia, the Counts Tasca, and other Marquis and Barons, but he was also the Don Calò who knew how to ride the wave of the new times, mixing business and politics, able to represent the peasants while defending the interests of the land owners. In 1901 he was already negotiating on behalf of the laborers with the owners for better contracts. Known as a strong supporter of social Catholicism, he put into practice the preachings of his uncle, the bishop, to "strengthen the old charities with the modern tools of social justice" when he created the "Cassa Rurale dei Prestiti Agrari" (Rural bank for agricultural credit). At the age of 41 during the First World War, Vizzini became rich through illegal speculation and cattle rustling. In 1918 he managed to sell about one hundred horses and mules he had stolen after having offered protection to the owners against theft.

In 1920 the laborers led by Socialists, war veterans, and Popular Party activists occupied the land of Belici at Villalba. The worried landowners asked Don Calò for his help in calming down the angry peasants and those who had just returned from the war who were demanding a parcel of land to start over. Vizzini acted as the mediator and in March 1921 Cavaliere Matteo Guccione, who owned the land, agreed to sell it for some three million lire to the laborers represented by Calogero Vizzini, his brother Don Salvatore as president of the "Cooperative of War Veterans of Villalba," and the Reverend Angelo Scarlata, president of the "Cassa Rurale San Giuseppe." The land was to be divided among the peasants but they actually had to pay rent for several years while the Cooperative became the temporary owner and collected some six thousand tons of wheat between 1921 and 1926 for the benefit of Calogero Vizzini. He also benefited from the final parceling of the former Belici property, buying thirty-eight acres for 70,000 lire. Another hefty share went to his sister Marietta, used as a stand-in for the Mafia boss.

As Fascism took over and following the appointment of Cesare Mori as prefect of Trapani, with the mission of "extirpating at the roots" any form of criminal activity to ensure the supremacy of the State on the island, many criminals decided to leave Sicily and seek their fortunes in the United States. Those who chose to stay had to endure Mori's harsh repression, which would relegate them to internal exile or to prisons run by the Fascist dictatorship. Mussolini gave the new prefect full power to engage in a quick and massive struggle against the Mafia. The Duce was well aware of the danger such an organization represented, even to the legitimacy of Fascism itself. In 1924, during a visit to Sicily, Mussolini became incensed when Don Ciccio Cuccia, the mayor of Piana degli Albanesi, an eccentric and tough Mafia boss, asked the head of the security service: "Tell me captain, why all these policemen? There is nothing to fear while I'm here. I'm the one who gives the orders here!" Back in Rome a furious Mussolini declared war on the criminal organization and gave Mori complete freedom of action. The prefect operated on a simple theory: to defeat the Mafia you had to be more of a mafioso than the mafiosi themselves. He therefore based his operations on the collaboration of the criminals, whether they were robbers or mafiosi. The collaboration he had in mind was to break through the wall of silence, called Omertà, by using torture, if required. Omertà was the main glue that kept the Honored Society together. The suspects were tied to a bed and forced to swallow salt water through a large funnel while their nose was held shut or to endure electric shocks to their genitals through a pedal-operated battery. The press published laudatory articles about Mori's work in Sicily, writing about "flowers that appeared miraculously whenever the patrols of the Iron Prefect went by."

In January 1926 at Ganci, a small village in the mountains of the Madonie, the territory of a mafia gang of Andaloro-Ferrarello and a favorite hiding place of many criminals, Mori made one of his most spectacular repressive forays by surrounding the village with hundreds of Carabinieri and militia men while ordering the water supply be interrupted and allowed no food supplier into town. If the criminals in hiding did not surrender the villagers would have died of thirst and hunger. The memory of those days lingers in the colorful recollections of the old timers:

> Whole families were taken hostage, including women and children, to force the Mafia leaders out of their hiding places. When they came out they were taken to the barracks where they were beaten and tortured to force them to talk. They had them drink salt water so it burned! They were all arrested and sent into exile whether they were guilty or not.

Mori made thousands of arrests in Sicily, including many untouchables like Giuseppe Genco Russo, the boss of Mussomeli. Even Don Calò experienced the anger of the "Iron Prefect" who accused him in 1928 of being the head of the so called "Mafia of the sulphur mines" and the man responsible for a "thick web of criminal ventures with even international ramifications responsible for a long series of obscure murders." The trial lasted three years and in January 1931 the Palermo Court acquitted Vizzini for lack of proof, thus confirming his status as a Mafioso who could hide any evidence that could be used against him. However he was sent into internal exile at Tricarico, a tiny village in the province of Lucania, where he remained until 1937.

Mussolini's tough tactics made the rounds all over the world. The *Times* of London praised the Duce for attacking the octopus in his homeland. Some New York newspapers were to write, "The Mafia is dead, a new Sicily is born." In 1927 Mussolini told parliament that the war against the Mafia had ended in total victory, calling the energetic prefect "the embodiment of the pure Fascist flame." In February 1928 Arnaldo Mussolini, the Duce's brother, published an article in *Il Popolo d'Italia* entitled "Sicily," where he emphatically proclaimed that the island was finally free of the Mafia.

In truth the Mafia was not dead at all. Many bandits and petty criminals had been relegated to internal exile, but few real Mafiosi had been locked up in jail and even fewer heads of gangs. Mori's actions had certainly managed to weaken the Mafia but they hadn't completely eradicated it. Many gangsters fled to the United States or to other countries or simply joined the Fascist Party. But that wasn't the end of it. Mori's repressive measures were criticized because of the brutal methods he used (but that Mussolini did not disapprove of) and the huge number of arrests in just four years. Eleven thousand people were thrown in jail under the suspicion of being Mafiosi, an alarming number that was even more of a problem because some arrests were made without drawing a line between gang leaders, soldiers, assassins, common criminals, thiefs, and bandits. The military head of the Italian army in Sicily, Antonio Di Giorgio, was extremely critical of the prefect's work and in a letter he sent to Mussolini on March 19, 1928, stated that it was not just the arbitrary nature of the arrests that was creating bitterness, but "the public's sense of fairness and justice has been aroused when an upper class gentleman was left untouched and who was also notoriously in contact with the Mafia and forced to be its protector. The poor illiterate man on the other hand was arrested only because under a death threat he delivered an anonymous letter. All this was very detrimental to the reputation of the regime… with the best educated and generous citizens distancing themselves" from the Fascist government itself.

Mussolini became convinced that the time had come to promote the prefect and transfer him out of Sicily, thereby ending his mission. Mori was therefore appointed a senator at the end of 1928. On June 23, 1929, Mussolini sent him the following telegram: "With a royal decree taking its course, Your Excellency has been placed in retirement in accordance to the number of years of service you have put in starting July 16. I thank you for your long and worthy service to the country."

While Mori was in Sicily Don Calogero Vizzini had not fled overseas, nor did he become a member of the Fascist Party. On the contrary, he managed to take an arm's-length attitude toward the Fascist government and to avoid the invitations of the party leaders in their black shirts to become a member of the Duce's extended political family. He expressed an opinion about becoming identified with Fascism: "Politicians, governments, and men in power change, while the Mafia stays the same." When the gang wars reached their peak in America in 1931 and Lucky Luciano had the two Sicilian-American bosses Masseria and Maranzano killed, thereby climbing to the top of the Mafia, Calogero Vizzini was being sent into internal exile far removed from his fiefdom of Villalba. This in no way prevented him from continuing to meet with his lieutenants and managing his illegal businesses.

Once the Mafia boss returned to Villalba he patiently waited for the foul atmosphere that still existed on the island to be swept away by the strong winds coming from the other side of the Atlantic. By the end of 1942 the American Mafia cousins and Lucky Luciano in particular, who viewed Calogero Vizzini as their only possible connection to quickly integrate the Honored Society and the new American Cosa Nostra, almost certainly found ways of informing the godfather of Villalba that the Americans were getting ready to land in Sicily and free the island from Fascist rule.

Chapter 3

The Underworld Project

The Collaboration Between Naval Intelligence and the Mafia

The official inquiry held by New York State Commissioner of Investigations, William B. Herlands, from January 28 to September 17, 1954, would offer proof that Charles Lucky Luciano and other top leaders of organized crime actively cooperated with the American war effort during World War II. Herlands was to demonstrate that an agreement had been reached between ONI and the head of the Italo-American Mafia, whereby the underworld would help the U.S. Navy protect New York Harbor from any act of sabotage perpetrated by German spies and Mussolini's sympathizers. This collaboration included the military planning of the landings in Sicily through contacts on the island that would help the offensive succeed in the occupied territories.

The Kefauver commission had questioned many gangsters close to Luciano and their lawyers, who had eloquently confirmed that the collaboration did in fact exist even though many details remained in the dark covered by the Mafia's code of silence—"omertà." Herlands went far beyond the Kefauver inquiry as he questioned many judges, prison personnel, big and small Mafia types, secret agents, and hundreds of other characters who were more or less known during those years, including a few members of Congress. The Navy also agreed to allow thirty-one officers to testify, besides some civilian personnel and enlisted men, under the condition that their testimony be given "top secret" classification.

For a long time the 101 pages of the Herlands Report and the 2,883 pages of accompanying signed testimony, along with the transcripts, files, phone taps, and other written proof remained under lock and key in a metal filing cabinet at the Navy Department. It was only during the mid-1970s, some thirty years after the end of World War II, that the Navy agreed to open its files and allow newsman Rodney Campbell to publish them in his book, *The Luciano Project.*[17]

A Pact with the Devil

On January 3, 1946, Lucky Luciano, the head of American organized crime and an inmate at Great Meadow penitentiary in Comstock near Albany, New York, received confirmation that the agreement reached four years before with the Office of Naval Intelligence was being carried out. On that day, following the request made by the New York State Board of Parole, Governor Thomas E. Dewey signed the authorization to free the Mafia boss by a commutation of sentence of extradition to Italy. On February 9 Luciano was taken aboard the cargo ship *Laura Keene* and set sail for Palermo.

The text of the commutation of Luciano's sentence written by Dewey stated:

---

17. Thomas Dewey asked William Herlands to conduct an investigation but the results were thought to be damaging to the U.S. Navy. Dewey kept the Herlands report locked with his other papers and it was released only after the former governor's death. See Richard Norton Smith, *Thomas E. Dewey and His Times* (New York: Simon and Shuster, 1982), pp. 573–74. [NDT]

On January 3, 1946, Governor Dewey announced that Lucky Luciano would be freed—not to remain in the United States but to be paroled to his birthplace in Sicily. "Upon the entry of the United States into the war Luciano's aid was sought by the armed services in inducing others to provide information concerning possible enemy attack. It appears that he cooperated in such efforts, though the actual value of the information provided is not clear. His record in prison is reported as wholly satisfactory."

Some years later, in an interview published in the *New York Post*, Dewey went a little further:

An exhaustive investigation…established that Luciano's aid to the Navy during the war was extensive and valuable. Ten years is probably as long as anybody ever served for compulsory prostitution. And these factors led the parole board to recommend the commutation, combined with the fact that Luciano would be exiled for life, under the law.[18]

By an odd twist of fate Dewey was the New York district attorney who had prosecuted Luciano in 1936 and with other young and ambitious lawyers he had led the battle against organized crime. Among the reasons for freeing Luciano, Dewey alluded to his collaboration with the U.S. Armed Forces, without entering into any details. He did not react when Congressman Walter Lynch accused him of "having acted unethically in commuting Luciano's sentence in order to allow his extradition."

A series of news investigations whipped up a storm after Lucky Luciano, in the course of one of the many chats with reporters he used to have in Naples cafés, said that he had contributed some $90,000 to the New York Republican Party for Thomas Dewey's presidential campaign. The newspapers published long stories intended to shed light on this obscure mystery that was to remain top secret for eight years until Dewey himself decided to quell the rumors and make public

---

18. Gosch and Hammer.

the evidence of the cooperation between organized crime and the armed forces of the United States.

Luciano had demanded immediate and unrestricted parole that would permit his return to New York to pick up the reins of empire. Dewey would have none of it. He agreed to work out a process for parole and freedom when he won the governorship but it would be granted only on condition that Luciano agree to his deportation to Italy and permanent exile from the United States.

I knew right away what that little mustached prick was gettin' at. In order for me to help him, and what's even more important not to go against him and hurt his chances to be President, the bastard was willin' to let me out—but he wanted me far, far away. That meant I'd have to agree to leave my own country, because I was a legal citizen ever since my old man took out papers when I was a kid. They couldn't deport me if I didn't agree to it. And I realized another thing he figured; it would make him look good that he was gettin' rid of that terrible gangster Lucky Luciano for the benefit of the United States of America.

But it meant somethin' else, too. It meant I'd have to stay in jail until the war was over. They couldn't send me to Italy while we was still at war and it was an enemy country. So, you see what happened? It's like guys tryin' to commit a perfect crime. I had worked up the perfect plan, I thought—and every goddamn point of it worked like a breeze, until Dewey come up with his condition. We argued like crazy, tryin' to get Dewey to change his mind, but it was no use. Dewey was standin' pat. Finally, I thought, what the hell—it was better than nothin'. At that point, it was a helluva lot better than rottin' in stir for years and tryin' to fight a losin' battle. Also, it occurred to me that maybe somethin' might happen later and I could find a way to get back after the war was over and everythin' cooled off. One thing, though; Dewey promised not to put the heat on the outfit like they did from 1939 to 1941. In other words, they could act sensible. And that's when I said okay, and all the fellas could sit down and work out the details.

Then we got to the price. Dewey got ninety grand from me. It was supposed to be a contribution to his governor's campaign. As a matter of fact, the way I remember it, he wanted a lot more. But the way I looked at it, that phony conviction of mine cost me so much money that Dewey oughta pay me to get out of the country. Besides, Costello didn't exactly forget that lovely double cross we got from the gentleman from Hyde Park and we wasn't about to shell out a big bundle in front, like before. We finally settled for twenty-five grand as a down payment. It was supposed to go into a secret Dewey campaign fund, and we agreed to put up the rest, the sixty-five thousand, when I got out. And we did pay it, in cash, in small bills, the minute I set foot on the boat that was gonna take me to Italy. You might say the cash was put in an escrow bag that was earmarked personally for Dewey's fund. Later on, I made a check about that ninety grand. It never showed on none of our books for tax returns, naturally; but it never showed up on none of Dewey's campaign returns either.[19]

A few days before William Herlands began his investigation a Republican congressman, William F. Horan, upset public opinion by stating that during the ten years he spent in the state penitentiary Lucky Luciano had been visited about forty times and eleven of these had been by Naval intelligence officers. Besides his family, the Mafia boss had also seen well-known lawyers, policemen, and well-known organized crime figures. The list that was published in the newspapers included: Frank Costello, Meyer Lansky, Socks Lanza, Bugsy Siegel, Willie Moretti, and Michele Lascari, while the visitor's log book always stated the same reasons.

At the request of naval intelligence, a private office was set aside for his conferences with Haffenden and with the steady stream of underworld visitors who poured in several times a week, supposedly involved with the top-secret Operation Underworld. Those conferences, however, dealt not with the war effort but with the mob's

---

19. Ibid.

own business, in gambling and black markets, and particularly with plans for the postwar years.[20]

The "Luciano case" erupted in the press just as forty-eight-year-old Judge Herlands was beginning his investigation. The questioning, cross examinations, sworn testimony, and deposition of all those involved in that intricate matter lasted eight months and the clerks of the commissioner of investigations produced three thousand typed pages of testimony. One person was not called as a witness, however—Lucky Luciano himself, who at the time was living in luxury hotels in Naples in the company of beautiful women.

With the understanding that the testimony of the navy officers involved would not be revealed, that testimony would be taken discreetly and the identity of secret agents and informers would not be made public, Herlands managed to obtain important information. Revealing testimony came from the defense lawyers for a few top New York mobsters who confirmed how certain gangsters being investigated "had opposed Axis forces with the same determination as the Navy, displaying a particular hatred toward Benito Mussolini."

The Hidden Truths

Between March 7, 1942, and May 1, 1944, some seventy-three U.S. Navy officers and eighty-two sailors and civilians in the Third Naval District that included New York, New Jersey, and Connecticut were engaged full time in operations.

Herlands had reached that conclusion some time before and a letter dated July 26, 1954, from Rear Admiral Carl F. Espe, head of the Office of Naval Intelligence at the Pentagon, provided further confirmation:

> During the spring of 1942, given Navy policy to exploit all potential sources of information, the head of the Military Intelligence Sector of the Third Naval District set up many intelligence networks of informers, many of whom had prior criminal records. One of these plans included contacting certain

---

20. Ibid.

criminal elements through the New York County District Attorney. At that time our country was beset by heavy losses at sea following enemy submarine attacks all along the Atlantic coast while the outcome of the war still appeared uncertain. There was also the worry of sabotage possibilities within the ports. It became necessary therefore to use any available means to prevent and prevent any supplies and potential contacts made with enemy submarines. To implement this project the Military Intelligence Section requested the transfer of Charles Lucky Luciano from Dannemora penitentiary to Great Meadow so that could be contacted more easily; the transfer took place on May 12, 1942. We know that immediately following, contacts were made with Luciano and that his influence on other criminal elements prompted their collaboration with Naval Intelligence that was thought to be useful to the Navy.

In his final report of September 17, 1954, Herlands wrote:

The facts indicate that Naval Intelligence secured and used the collaboration of Luciano within the constantly changing and increasing picture of national security requirements…. undoubtedly Luciano with his colleagues and contacts at a time when the fortunes of war seemed very uncertain, provided a wide range of services that the Navy found useful.

Operation Underworld

Between late December 1941 and February 1942 the U.S. Navy had suffered heavy losses. In the Atlantic some seventy-one cargo ships had been sunk by German U-boats. Most of these ships were headed to England with all kinds of weapons and supplies. It was an unbearable situation for the Joint Chiefs of Staff, who were convinced they would win the war in Europe but that the victory could be thwarted if Allied shipping kept on being destroyed as it traveled across the Atlantic. The Third District of Naval Intelligence, which included the port of New York and the East Coast of the United

States, was not performing properly. The head of the Third District, Roscoe C. McFall, had clearly described the task to the Herlands Commission, namely to obtain from any potential source information so that other sections of the Navy could take appropriate action to prevent or fight as required anything that could interfere with the transport of troops, supplies, and munitions and to secure the port and every other section that was part of the Third Naval District.

I had a newspaper with me and I showed them how the Navy Department was givin' out a lot of stories about sabotage and fifth column and that kind of thing. There was even a story on the front page about a campaign they called "Zip Your Lip," which shows how worried they was about German subs sinkin' our ships or some spies blowin' up ships in the harbor. It looked like the whole Eastern waterfront, especially in New York, was a mess of sabotage.[21]

How was it possible that information regarding convoys about to set sail out of New York harbor could reach the Germans? Charles Radcliffe Haffenden, who was in command of the investigative section of the Third Naval District B-3, known as the Ferret Squad, felt that information about the movement of convoys and the refueling and supplying of submarines originated with criminal elements of German or Italian origin operating within the metropolitan area. According to that line of thinking, those individuals could provide information to the enemy for nationalistic reasons; it was also possible that some who had been involved in bootlegging during Prohibition may have found new sources of revenue selling contraband supplies and fuel to enemy submarines.

The Navy was deeply concerned at that moment about the New York waterfront. Many of the businessmen there and many of the dock workers were Italians and Sicilians—a majority immigrants or sons of immigrants. Thus their loyalty to the United States came under question and there was fear that they might incite strikes or commit acts that would seriously affect the war effort, that they might even use

---

21. Ibid.

their fishing boats to carry information and supplies to German sub-marine packs lying offshore.[22]

On March 7, 1942, the new New York County district attorney, Frank S. Hogan (who had replaced Dewey as of January 1, 1942), urgently called a meeting with the heads of Naval Intelligence to discuss the delicate issue of the port of New York, which was by now an open secret. From his office on Leonard Street, Hogan called in Capt. McFall, Lt. O'Malley, Cdr. Haffenden, Assistant D.A. Murray I. Gurfein, the head of the Rackets Bureau, and other responsible persons, including Lt. Anthony J. Marzullo, who would later change his name to Marsloe and who would be one of the first Americans to land at Gela, in Sicily, on July 10, 1943. Marsloe was fluent in the Sicilian dialect and became the most active recruiter of gangsters for counterintelligence operations. Reluctant at first to involve organized crime in military matters, he was persuaded by an old FBI friend, John O'Connell, who told him quite candidly: "What's involved is the survival of the United States. We must use every tool we have within the armed forces and government agencies for the war effort to succeed."

The meeting in the D.A.'s office had a single point on its agenda: to put a stop to the information that flowed from New York to the desks of German officers in Berlin that had decimated the U.S. Navy in a few short months. Just one month before that meeting, on February 9, the former luxury flagship of the French Line, the *Normandie* (renamed *Lafayette*), had caught fire as it was being turned into a troop transport ship that could carry up to ten thousand soldiers. After some twelve hours the ship had capsized on its side in the icy waters of the Hudson River, ending its short career as one of the fastest transatlantic liners. The art deco restaurants, the luxury suites, the magnificent theater were all engulfed in flames in a terrible sight for the tens of thousands of New Yorkers looking on at the water's edge. The investigation concluded that it was an accidental mishap due to the negligence of a few workmen who were adapting the ship as a troop transport. However, Hogan was convinced that there had to be something else behind the *Normandie* incident and the question remained open. None of those taking part in the meeting could come

---

22. Ibid.

up with a satisfactory answer. Many people thought that Hitler's secret agents were behind the sabotage while others were more inclined to believe that organized crime was behind it in order to prove the harbor was not safe and that it therefore needed the Mafia's protection.

When Lucky Luciano dictated his book, *Last Testament of Lucky Luciano*, to Martin Gosch twenty years later and remembered that spectacular act of sabotage in New York harbor, he said it was basically the idea of Meyer Lansky's, the "little man." Lansky mentioned that something big, looking like sabotage was going to happen soon, so big that the Navy or someone else would be compelled to ask the Mafia bosses to provide protection. The *Normandie* on the West Side docks in Manhattan was the perfect set up. If anything happened to that ocean liner Naval intelligence would be caught off, guard as Luciano remembered:

> Albert said that the guys from Navy intelligence had been all over the docks talkin' to 'em about security; they was scared to death that all the stuff along the Hudson, the docks and boats and the rest, was in very great danger. It took a guy like Albert to figure out somethin' really crazy; his idea was to give the Navy a real big hunk of sabotage, somethin' so big that it would scare the shit out of the whole fuckin' Navy. This big French luxury ship, the *Normandie*, was sittin' at a pier on the West Side of Manhattan, and accordin' to what Tony and Albert was told, the government was workin' out a deal with that guy de Gaulle to take it over and turn it into a troopship. Albert figures that if somethin' could happen to the *Normandie* that would really make everybody crap in their pants.[23]

The newspapers whipped up a storm of accusations against the Navy's inability to protect the harbor, demanding immediate assistance to put an end to potential acts of sabotage. Even Italian and Sicilian dock workers protested the situation but their loyalty to the United States was called into question and they were singled out as possible spies for the Fascist government. A pervasive atmosphere of chaos was created in New York harbor and the Navy decided to launch Operation Underworld. At Third District headquarters on 90 Church

---

23. Ibid.

Street, Haffenden was given the task of setting up contacts with organized crime. He immediately created a team that included FBI agents, detectives, investigators from the D.A.'s office, Treasury Department officers, and lawyers, besides the Naval Intelligence operatives. All were asked to wear uniforms. The archives of the Rackets Bureau turned out to be an excellent source of information for the operation.

During a second meeting with District Attorney Hogan, Haffenden brought of his two closest collaborators with him, O'Malley and Marsloe, in order to use not just the foot soldiers of the organized crime syndicate but most of all their leaders in obtaining intelligence that would be useful to the Navy. Contact would be made indirectly through their lawyers. Haffenden was not only interested in the Sicilians of the old Mafia, whom Mussolini had expelled from Italy during the 1920s and who had escaped to America, but was also thinking mostly of the bosses who were currently active and in control of the people and merchandise moving around the port of New York. The most important player in the fish market in the eastern United States was Joe "Socks" Lanza, who controlled that industry and its related rackets. He was known as the "czar of the docks" who obeyed only one man: Lucky Luciano. Lanza was the right person to kick off Operation Underworld. Lanza's lawyer Joseph Guerin, was summoned to Haffenden's office and told what the Navy was up against. In the month of May alone, said Haffenden, the Germans had sunk fifty allied ships, twenty-four of them American, out of New York Harbor. He was convinced that German submarines were being supplied with food and fuel in U.S. waters through fishing boats and they had to be stopped.

Lanza agreed to a meeting, but only if it was held in private—a public meeting could make trouble for him, he said, if word got around that he was seen talking to someone in uniform. So a rendezvous was set for midnight on a park bench at Grant's Tomb on the upper West Side of Manhattan. Haffenden asked for Lanza's help in combating sabotage and fifth columnists. Specifically, he wanted Lanza to permit naval intelligence to install sophisticated communications equipment and place agents in the fish market and aboard fishing boats. Lanza said he would help all he could in the market, but he told Haffenden, as he had been rehearsed, that he had no power over the docks or over the other areas the government might want to monitor. If the government really wanted to get the entire Italian-Sicilian population cooperating fully, and especially if it wanted the help of the underworld, there was only one man to see. Haffenden asked for the name. Lanza told him—Charlie Lucky Luciano, currently an inmate at Dannemora prison.[24]

The lawyer answered without hesitation: "I'm sure Lanza will agree to help you." Haffenden was also careful to say that Socks would draw no advantage in exchange for his help because he would only be doing his "patriotic duty."

Lanza and Haffenden were to meet at the Astor Hotel on Broadway, where the commander kept a small private office. Lanza confirmed that he was making himself available, adding that "I'm in one hundred percent." Haffenden asked Lanza to infiltrate some of his agents among the men working in the fishing industry, most of them Italo-Americans all along the eastern seaboard. In order to avoid creating any suspicion they would have to be hired regularly and become members of the union. Lanza was to arrange this personally. Socks gave assurances that "It can be done." But he added that if the government really wished to secure the cooperation of the Sicilian immigrants and especially of organized crime, then they needed to talk to the boss of bosses, meaning Lucky Luciano.

The Agreement Between Lucky Luciano and Naval Intelligence

Assistant District Attorney Murray Gurfein phoned Lucky Luciano's attorney Moses Polakoff to set up a meeting with the boss, who was an inmate in Dannamora State Prison. Polakoff answered that it was best to have a preliminary meeting where he could bring a close friend of Luciano's who could then persuade the other underworld bosses. Without naming anyone he made a date with Gurfein to have breakfast the next morning in a fashionable restaurant on East 58th

---

24. Ibid.

Street in Manhattan. A slight man with dark hair accompanied him when the Assistant D.A. arrived.

"Mr. Gurfein, this is Meyer Lansky," said Polakoff.

This came as a shock to Gurfein. Meyer Lansky had been for many years, and still was, the head of the New York rackets. At the end of the 1920s he had been Bugsy Siegel's partner in running the infamous Bugs and Meyer Mob, an "association" of sorts whose main business was homicide. In the early 1930s they had worked with Frank Costello, Joe Adonis, Louis "Lepke" Buchalter, Owney Madden, Lucky Luciano, and Joe "The Boss" Masseria. They had made millions of dollars with Luciano and Adonis in smuggling liquor and after the repeal of Prohibition even more money in illegal gambling.

Gurfein was nervous that someone could spot the head of the Rackets Division sitting quietly with a notorious extortionist and criminal. Without providing any specifics he explained to Lansky why he needed to see the Italian-American boss. Lansky answered Gurfein that Luciano could be interested and that he would be more useful if he were out of jail. They had to talk to him but Dannemora was a waste of time: it was way too far upstate and it took two days to make the round trip to New York City. What should be done immediately was to transfer Luciano to a facility closer to the city. Either Sing Sing, for example, which was very close, or Great Meadow in Comstock, near Albany. Gurfein agreed and quickly left, anxious to get away from both Polakoff and Lansky.

Luciano later suggested to Haffenden that it would be a lot easier for him to make contributions to national defense if he were not confined in Dannemora, so far from everyone he knew and would have to confer with. He told Haffenden he would need to have constant contact with his friends in New York and around the country, to talk personally with couriers who would pass on his orders to the hierarchy of his nationwide organization. Among those he had to see constantly, he said, were Lansky, Costello, Lanza, Albert Anastasia, and Tony Anastasio, Adonis, and several others.

On May 12, 1942, Luciano and eight other inmates left the penitentiary at Dannemora to be transferred to Great Meadow. There it was easier for Gurfein to convince the warden, Vernon Morhous, to authorize meetings between ONI officers and many of the boss's "friends" without taking their fingerprints on the official visitor's log book. A few days later Luciano was taken from his cell to the warden's office where he found his lawyer Moses Polakoff and Meyer Lansky. Luciano was surprised to see Lansky whom he had not seen in years. "What the hell are you doing here?" was all he could say. Then, once the surprise wore off Lansky and Polakoff began to fill Luciano in on the most recent events. They said that "Socks" Lanza was doing the best he could but needed Luciano's help so that the cooperation with ONI could work properly.

"We're here to find out if you'll help the Navy," said Lansky, "and we think you should." Luciano gave it some thought then said: "O.K. I'll help them." But he also added that nobody knew when this war would end and that when he had been sent to the penitentiary he was also handed a deportation notice and thought that some day he'd have to return to Italy. He wanted to live there in peace.

If the Italians found out that I helped the U.S. Navy during the war I'd be a dead man. They'd kill me. Nobody in Sicily must find out what I'm doing.

As far as Haffenden was concerned, he didn't know nothin' that was goin' on except that he was sittin' there with his mouth open, prayin' I would say yes and help his whole department down at 90 Church Street. Finally I said, yes, and I could see him let out a big sigh of relief. He was a very happy guy. The Dewey's guy suggested that Haffenden go into another office and call his people at naval intelligence, so that we would have a chance to confer on the details of how this would be worked out.

When the kid left the room, that's when we got down to cases. We put it right on the table. I said that the way we figured it, after Wilkie beat Dewey for the Republican presidential nomination in 1940, Dewey had to win the governorship of New York in order to get in line for another shot at the nomination. Costello chimed in and said he'd already gotten word that the Republican big shots had agreed to push Dewey for President in 1944 even though he was runnin' for governor on the promise not to try for President in two years.

I repeated my promise that Dewey would get all our support and we would deliver Manhattan, or come damn close, in November, which would mean he'd be a shoo-in. Then, as soon as he got into office, he hadda make me a hero. The only difference would be, a hero gets a medal, but I'd get a parole…

Lansky reassured him

"Absolutely Charlie. Everybody wants to keep quiet about all this."

Then Luciano asked that they send up Socks Lanza to see him. Later he explained:

In order for me to help him [Dewey], and what's even more important not to go against him and hurt his chances to be President, the bastard was willin' to let me out—but he wanted me far, far away.

The last day on Ellis Island, Lansky and me had a meet, just the two of us. I told him somethin' that none of the other guys knew up to that point—that I had already made connections in Italy to get visas under my real name, Salvatore Lucania, that would be good for Cuba and Mexico and a whole lotta countries in South America. I told Meyer I figured it would take me about six months of layin' low, gettin' adjusted in Italy, and makin' personal contacts instead of havin' guys front for me. I said that if there was gonna be any problem for me to get back into the United States, I'd even be willin' to become a Cuban citizen, and then take back control from there.

The partnership between Naval intelligence and the Mafia was sealed. Operation Underworld, the strangest intelligence and counter-intelligence undertaking of the Second World War, had reached its operational stage. On June 4, 1942, Luciano had his first meeting with Lanza. The Herlands investigation established that those meetings at Great Meadow were an "event of prime importance" to the success of the operation. In his testimony before the Herlands investigation

Lanza revealed the names of the persons that Luciano asked him to contact: Joe Adonis, Frank Costello, the Camarda brothers, Albert Anastasia, Jack Parisi, Anthony Romeo, Willie Moretti, Mike Lascari, Johnny "Crosseye" Dunn (head of the International Longshoremen's Association and a friend of Joseph Ryan, who controlled the Hudson River docks). Luciano was very clear in speaking with Lanza: "Tell them I'm behind this. Use my name and you'll have no problems."

Everybody went to work for the Navy. Luciano was able to stitch together the organization's connections and the agreement between organized crime and Naval intelligence was advantageous to both parties: the Navy could guarantee the safety of the convoys on their way to Europe; the Mafia tightened its control of the waterfront. The mere presence of those individuals on the docks was enough to discourage anyone from attempting to commit acts of sabotage. In his testimony to the Herlands Commission Lansky clearly discussed the tasks given to Johnny Dunn, who was to be a watchdog on the docks, get reliable people among the stevedores to keep an eye on the doubtful ones, meaning those who could possibly engage in sabotage or talk too much. He would order his men to make friends in the bars in front of the docks and report back on anyone who was talking too much or looked like a subversive.

Meyer Lansky became Luciano's arms and legs in Operation Underworld and he met with Haffenden at the Astor Hotel with increasing frequency. Lansky carefully checked the loading and unloading operations of the ships and also tried to stop any strike moves by the longshoremen. His visits to Luciano went on for several months. Through many meetings with Lansky and Lanza in the comfortable and private offices of the prison warden the boss started to give orders that had less to do with the Navy's problems.

On August 25, 1942, Luciano even had a meeting in prison with Frank Costello, the slot machine king, and eight other persons. A formal Mafia summit took place inside the State prison that lasted some three hours. Luciano and the work done by his group was fast becoming essential to the Navy; however, while the Mafia was delivering on its end of the secret agreement, on the other end the boss was able to maintain his control over illegal activity. This would all be confirmed in the phone taps Frank Hogan had ordered on Socks Lanza's phone line at the Meyer's Hotel. The transcripts of those conversations often carried embarrassing information—as for example those with ONI Commander Haffenden, who praised the work of specific gangsters. In some phone calls Lanza was recorded promising Haffenden some excellent fresh fish and other seafood at Fulton's Fish Market or, if he preferred, lobster and crab

At the end of 1942 the cooperation between organized crime and the Navy reached its apex. Even Haffenden was viewed as a mysterious and charismatic character by the Mafia. To be working for the Commander had become a password on the docks, on the fishing boats, in restaurants and nightclubs, and even within the union itself. Only a select few had any idea that the "Commander" was a Naval officer. Lansky explained that the Commander needed men to take on certain tasks and provided the right man for the job. The man then worked only for Haffenden and Lansky did not know what the fellow would be doing. Only the Commander knew that.

Haffenden could also count on 50 officers and 81 military and civilian agents, all of them involved in secret operations. The results of the cooperation with organized crime became immediately apparent. In June 1942 eight German saboteurs were able to disembark from two U-boats on the coast of Long Island and near Jacksonville, Florida, but were quickly apprehended by the FBI. Some fishing boats had sighted the submarines and Haffenden had taken part in the operation with Paul Alfieri and Anthony Marsloe. Any strikes on the waterfront were nipped in the bud and the would-be organizers were unable to carry out any protest because of growing pressure from intimidation, firing, and in some cases physical elimination. Following the agreement between the Mafia and Naval intelligence, some thirty homicides that took place on the waterfront could almost certainly be attributed to the secret pact. However, for the rest of the war there were to be no further acts of sabotage on the New York waterfront.

As Lt. Kelley was to testify, there were no further acts of sabotage and more importantly there was no loose talk by stevedores, porters, or shipshandlers about the kind of goods that were being loaded or unloaded and their destination. This was of prime importance since enemy agents wanted to find out all these details and the Navy's job was to prevent them from doing so.

Naval Intelligence (ONI) and the Landings in Sicily

At the end of 1942 the excellent results by ONI at the port of New York prompted the heads of the Third Naval District to use the agreement with organized crime in their plans for the occupation of Sicily. To prepare for the landings, detailed information was required and the best sources were precisely the Mafiosi who had escaped during the Mori period. At the same time an Italian Section of Secret Intelligence had already been created within the OSS under a young Sicilian-American named Max Biagio Corvo, a native of the town of Melilli. Corvo had already been working on an intelligence plan for the occupation of the island that called for the recruitment of anti-Fascist elements in the United States and elsewhere who had escaped from Italy following the March on Rome in 1922. The idea was to subvert the Fascist state through the operations of U.S. intelligence. The Third Naval District therefore began focusing on that island in the Mediterranean.

Naval intelligence Section F (foreign intelligence) of ONI began operating in December 1942 under the name "Target Section." Its mission was strategic counterintelligence and as of May 11, 1943, it was focusing on the Mediterranean and North Africa. Commander Haffenden was in charge of the unit, with Lt. Commander Harold W. McDowell as his deputy. The team included men who had already worked on intelligence matters relating to organized crime in the United States and naval officers who could speak Italian, particularly the Sicilian dialect. Kathleen Mitchell was one of the few women to work with Haffenden in the archives section. The map section, the true center of F Section, was located at 50 Church Street in lower Manhattan, a top-secret location under constant guard by the Marines.

George M. Tarbox, a painter, cartographer, and civil servant was in charge of maps and had been working for the Third District since February 1942. On very short notice he was able to create a 4' x 6' map of Sicily mounted on a wooden easel. On the cellophane overleaf

Tarbox would draw in black ink the various strategic targets: airports, industrial and military installations, coastlines, roadbeds, and anything related to enemy positions.

Even prior to the creation of F Section and the Casablanca Conference in January 1943, when Roosevelt and Churchill officially decided to attack Italy, starting with the invasion of the Sicilian coast, Haffenden's men had assembled a large amount of material concerning the island. Most of it came from papers that had been forgotten in the attics of the many Sicilian immigrants who were now ready to open their heirlooms to help the American war effort. Sicilian-Americans had been approached directly by ONI headquarters but those requests were not very successful. Those who did respond were astonished when navy clerks asked them to see photographs and postcards of the various Mediterranean ports where they originally came from. These were street- and sea-level photographs offering a much more realistic view of the beaches and areas where the landings were to take place; they were used for the identification of the target beaches and port installations.

Lieutenant Marsloe, who also doubled as an interpreter, remembered during one of his last television interviews:

> I was mostly interested in the pictures and names of their relatives back in Italy, where they lived and what they did for a living. They gave us whatever they could. Some of them were hostile and I'd tell them that America was the land where they were making a living, where they owned a house and therefore owed it their livelihood. It was their duty to do anything they could to save an American boy's life.

The suspicion the immigrants showed when approached by naval officers was preventing an effective search for information about the island. Haffenden then went to the list of Sicilian-American gangsters who had worked with him in breaking any sabotage that was taking place in New York Harbor. Many of the mobsters were born in Sicily and knew their native land better than anyone else in the United States. Some still had friends and relatives on the island and disliked the

Fascist government that had forced them to leave. Those same gangsters managed to convince the immigrants to help ONI, and the key man to do this was once again Lucky Luciano. On his signal any kind of information about Sicily would find its way to Haffenden's desk. In his testimony to the Herlands Commission Roscoe McFall said that before the landings in North Africa and even later, the intelligence section of the Third District was focused on collecting strategic information about North Africa and the Mediterranean. The assumption was that Mussolini had expelled many Sicilians and they would therefore be inclined to help. Haffenden had numerous reports showing how his men were interviewing a lot of native-born Italians and that they were cooperating because of Lucky Luciano.

From Great Meadow penitentiary the Sicilian boss became irreplaceable to American intelligence operations during an important phase of World War II operations. Once again Moses Polakoff acted as the go-between for Haffenden and Luciano. He arranged several meetings of Italian-Americans at Haffenden's office with photographs, books, letters, and documents regarding their cities of origin in Sicily.

According to Haffenden's secretary, Kathleen Mitchell, in her testimony to the Herlands Commission, Haffenden had many phone conversations and received innumerable old books and a mass of information that had to be analyzed. The people in Haffenden's office examined all this material hoping to find useful data.

Haffenden went directly to Meyer Lansky, who followed Luciano's information and identified the man who could actually help ONI solve the lack of specific information about Sicily. This was the illegal gambling organizer Joe Adonis, who had been arrested several times for bootlegging, extortion, kidnapping, and various degrees of assault. Haffenden asked Adonis to perform tasks that had been decided by Meyer Lansky, as he testified to the Herlands Commission. Adonis kept in contact with Italians who could be of help to the Navy. Lansky would tell Adonis what to look for and Adonis ferreted out some Italians who were not U.S. citizens and took them to Church Street. Haffenden wanted Italians with a knowledge of Sicily and the islands close by, and who still had relatives there. Adonis could help in providing such individuals and bringing them to Haffenden so he could make corrections on the many maps he had. Haffenden also wanted postcards of ports and harbors, as well as the exact configuration of the coastline. There were also people who had fled Italy because they were Freemasons, among them a former mayor who had been contacted through Lucky Luciano and provided more contacts to other Sicilians.

Did Lucky Luciano Land in Sicily?

At the beginning of 1943 all American military intelligence was focused on the landings in Sicily. The OSS had already set up the team that was supposed to land first and make contacts in Italy for the political and administrative structure of the occupied territories. Haffenden was assembling all kinds of information and creating files on hundreds of names. The collaboration with Luciano was working well. The Third District commanding officer came up with an idea: free the boss and send him along with other agents into Sicily to prepare the American invasion. The Herlands Commission was unable to uncover any information regarding this strange story, even though to this day there are still those who say they saw Luciano in the streets of Palermo in the first few months of 1943.

Haffenden discussed his idea with McFall, the head of counter intelligence who stated in his testimony that at the end of 1942, after the landings in North Africa but before the invasion of Sicily, Luciano's name was mentioned. Haffenden said that Luciano was ready to go to Sicily to make contact with local people and convince them to help the American war effort, especially during the amphibious landings. According to Luciano Haffenden was also ready to provide information about the territory and the fortifications. McFall remembered that Haffenden had a plan to free the Mafia chieftain from jail, provide him with the necessary papers, and to infiltrate Sicily through a neutral country, such as Portugal. This would require that Haffenden contact Governor Thomas E. Dewey of New York and obtain a pardon for Luciano and that the importance of Luciano's help justified freeing him from prison. Haffenden insisted that this be done immediately.

Haffenden told McFall that Luciano had already agreed to the plan and said the boss had indicated that the Gulf of Castellammare near Palermo, was the best location for a landing and that the military chiefs at Casablanca had considered the location for the same purpose. McFall verbally told his superiors of the proposal but advised that they should "forget the whole thing because it would discredit the entire U.S. Navy." Even though top ONI officers were already collaborating with the Mafia for military reasons, McFall felt that it was unthinkable that the United States should free a Mafioso as important as Lucky Luciano.

To confirm that the United States judiciary system would not agree to any kind of bargain, on January 29, 1943, a sentence was signed by Judge James Garrett Wallace against Joe Socks Lanza, the man who more than any other had collaborated with the ONI in the early days of sabotage in New York harbor. Lanza received seven to fifteen years for his part in an extortion scheme relating to New York City taxi drivers.

Haffenden's comment about the judge recorded in a wire tap was clear: "That a son of a bitch...!"

Luciano Requests His Freedom

Three days after Socks Lanza was found guilty George H. Wolf, one of Luciano's attorneys, filed a request for the commutation of the sentence imposed in 1936 on his client, Charles Lucky Luciano. Judge Philip McCook, who had originally sentenced the Mafia boss, examined the request. In his request Wolf underlined Luciano's excellent conduct in prison and purposely omitted any mention of his collaboration with the ONI and the many "favors" the gangster had provided to American intelligence. The two attorneys thought it was best they avoid, at least for the moment, having his collaboration become public knowledge, and limited themselves to a few allusions in court that Judge McCook immediately cut short by saying that he was "ready to discuss those matters in private." Both Haffenden and Gurfein were also called in to testify and didn't provide any details regarding Luciano's collaboration nor any details of the help he may have given to the ONI. Haffenden would have liked to help Luciano but his superior, Captain McFall, decided that the Navy should under no circumstances be involved in reducing Luciano's sentence. Haffenden strictly followed his orders, making the rejection of the commutation a forgone conclusion.

On February 10, 1943, Judge McCook issued a ruling that was considered controversial. He rejected Luciano's request but also mentioned that on the issue of the defendant's cooperation in the war effort, after asking the authorities repeatedly and confidentially, the court was satisfied that the defendant successfully helped the authorities but that this did not allow the court to entertain the request. The defendant, he said, was cooperating with the authorities and continued to do so by having exemplary conduct in prison. An act of clemency could be considered in the future by the executive branch.

Judge McCook's decision left Luciano with the hope that he could be free but the Mafia chieftain would have to wait a few more years to get out of jail. According to Luciano the terms of the secret agreements he entered with the heads of ONI did not state that the judges would reject his request for the commutation of his sentence. The story he told Martin Gosch included a statement that he provided Dewey with large contributions to the New York gubernatorial campaign and his run for the presidency in 1944. In exchange once he became governor, Dewey agreed to parole him.

Luciano had demanded immediate and unrestricted parole that would permit his return to New York to pick up the reins of empire. Dewey would have none of it. He agreed to work out a process for parole and freedom when he won the governorship, but it would be granted only on condition that Luciano agree to his deportation to Italy and permanent exile from the United States. [25]

The Mafia boss understood that his deportation would have been good for Dewey's image because the governor would get credit for ridding the United States of a terrible gangster. But there was more to the story. According to Luciano the deal was that he was to stay in jail until the war was over.

---

25. Ibid.

The request for a commutation of sentence came far too early, according to the alleged agreement with Dewey. In his *Last Testament* Luciano said the only thing to do was to wait patiently for the war to end before even thinking of getting out. Following McCook's negative ruling, Luciano withdrew a bit from collaborating with the ONI. The visits at Great Meadow became rare and some of his most trusted friends like Frank Costello, no longer traveled up to see him. The New York waterfront was in any case under tight control and during that time there were neither acts of sabotage nor strikes of any kind. Joe Adonis in particular became one of Haffenden's most active collaborators by consolidating the relationship with hundreds of informers among Italian-Americans and within organized crime. The Herlands Commission report indicates that at that time the main go-between Adonis used was Vincenzo Mangano. He was one of the most influential import and export traffickers between the United States and Italy and one who could count on many contacts and connections. Mangano also traded in cheese, olives, wine, and olive oil and was said to be one of the main contacts between the New York and Sicilian Mafias and brought information back and forth across the Atlantic. He was more than happy to do Mussolini harm and provided hundreds of informers to that effect.

Mangano kept in close touch with his native land and when he was asked whether he brought Lucky Luciano to Sicily he would answer with tears welling up in his eyes: "Luciano in Sicily? It was high time that someone should go there to straighten things out in the Mafia."

From 1942 to 1946 Luciano remained officially an inmate at Com—stock and in his *Last Testament* the boss denied any kind of agreement with the intelligence agencies regarding his providing assistance for the landings in Sicily:

> But as far as my helpin' the government was concerned, then or even the following year when they said I helped 'em open up Sicily for the invasion by gettin' the cooperation of the Mafia guys to help the American troops, that was all horseshit. It would be easy for me to say there was somethin' to all that, like people have been sayin' for years and I've been lettin' 'em think, but there wasn't. As

far as me helpin' the army land in Sicily, you gotta remember I left there when I was, what—nine? The only guy I knew real well over there, and he wasn't even Sicilian, was that little prick Vito Genovese. In fact, at that time the dirty little bastard was livin' like a king in Rome, kissin' Mussolini's ass.[26]

The newspapers kept on printing stories about the rejection of the request for parole for Lucky Luciano and many commentators were openly favorable to Judge McCook for letting the head of the Italian-American Mafia rot in jail. Newsmen were most of all interested in the connection between organized crime and the ONI that had suddenly become public knowledge.

And then the war in Europe was over. On the very day it ended, May 7, 1945, a petition for executive clemency and freedom for Charles Lucania was sent to Governor Thomas E. Dewey. He quickly turned the matter over to the state parole board, whose members were all his appointees. Luciano's attorneys told the board he "has cooperated with high military authorities. He has rendered a definite service to the war effort." And so he should be freed. Haffenden wrote a personal letter lauding Luciano for his efforts, which, he said, had helped shorten the war in Sicily and Italy. Precisely what those efforts had been, the board was not told; Haffenden did not say and the Navy refused to reveal details.

On January 3, 1946, Governor Dewey announced that Lucky Luciano would be freed—not to remain in the United States but to be paroled to his birthplace in Sicily. "Upon the entry of the United States into war," Dewey said, "Luciano's aid was sought by the armed services in inducing others to provide information concerning enemy attack. It appears that he cooperated in such efforts, though the actual value of the information provided is not clear. His record in prison is reported as wholly satisfactory."

At the same time knowledge of the agreements brought to light the state of confusion that characterized U.S. intelligence. Within the ONI section that was working on research on Sicily some operatives had been kept in the dark regarding the agreement with the Mafia: the men

---

26. Ibid.

of Section B7-I ("I" standing for Italy) in Washington under the command of Marine Corps Colonel Angelo J. Cincotta. No memorandum or piece of information had reached his desk even though his office was in charge of assembling information about Italy. Cincotta knew nothing of the assistance provided by Lanza or Luciano; he didn't know that they controlled the waterfront nor about the strategic information the Sicilian immigrants provided and the lists of friends they could count on in Sicily itself. Cincotta was amazed when he read the *New York Times* on the morning of February 11, 1943, and traveled to New York to investigate but was unable to find out any information at all. He only learned that his superiors, including the head of Naval intelligence in Washington, D.C., Admiral Arthur Train, were aware of the matter. They probably needed to have some staff officer able to testify in good faith, in the event an investigation was initiated, that he had no knowledge of any agreements with organized crime and specifically with Lucky Luciano. In fact Cincotta's testimony to the Herlands Commission was that ONI headquarters was informed in 1943 that Charles Luciano had presented to Judge Philip McCook a request for commutation of his sentence accompanied by statements to the effect that Luciano had been of assistance to the person responsible for intelligence in the District by providing crucially important information about Sicily and Italy, including the names of other informers. Cincotta was immediately dispatched to New York to investigate the role played by the Intelligence division in the Third District and what initiatives had been taken to support the request for commutation of sentence presented by Luciano. Cincotta stated that no information obtained by Luciano and his informers about operations in Sicily ever reached his desk at the Navy Department in Washington.

Luciano's lawyer, Moses Polakoff, in one of his many depositions in front of the Herlands Commission, was able to shed light on some details that remained unclear after the investigation. When asked how Luciano, who had lived in the United States since childhood, could have information vital to the American war effort, Polakoff answered that all he could say was what Haffenden had told him and did not know whether others were aware of it as well. Polakoff did not think

Luciano could do much from prison but apparently Italians were very faithful to certain traditions and held certain individuals that they obeyed in very high esteem. The ONI and other authorities felt that Luciano was one of those individuals. He was viewed as powerful and influential within the Italian community.

When it was suggested that the Mafia boss or even he, Polakoff, had in fact organized the whole matter, the latter replied that the idea that a man like Luciano could be of some help did not originate with him (Luciano) or his lawyer, but came directly from Naval intelligence or from others who were providing information to the ONI and felt that Luciano could be useful, as he appears to have been.

In exile in Italy Luciano remained very mysterious about his collaboration with U.S. intelligence. In the course of an interview with United Press he said: "I wasn't let out of jail because of any particular help I gave to the United States during the war but only because the American courts understood that I was absolutely innocent."

Commissioner Herlands in his final report dated September 17, 1954, asked two questions and answered both unhesitatingly: had the Armed Forces asked for Luciano's help to persuade others to come forward with information about potential enemy attacks? Did Luciano collaborate in these efforts? Herlands' answer in both cases was "Decidedly, yes."

The Kefauver Commission investigates organized crime in 1950.
Frank Costello testifies at the far end of the table.

above
Costello testifies.

left
The *Normandie* on its side after the suspicious fire that destroyed it on Pier 88 on the Hudson River, February 9, 1942.

below
New York D.A. Thomas E. Dewey *(right)* with Assistant D.A. Murray I. Gurfein during the trial of Lucky Luciano in 1936.

right
Capt. Roscoe MacFall.

below
Commander Charles R. Haffenden, head of the Third
Naval District, in his office at the Astor Hotel, 1942.

Frank Costello, police mug shot, 1935.

Charles "Lucky" Luciano, police mug shot, 1936.

Meyer Lansky, police mug shot, 1931.

Vito Genovese, police mug shot, 1935.

Joe "Socks" Lanza, 1940.

above
Chicago police lineup on April 19, 1935. *From the left:* Paul Ricca, Sylvester Agoglia, Charles "Lucky" Luciano, Meyer Lansky, John Senna, and Harry Brown.

right
Alphonse "Al" Capone.

Defense attorney Moses Polakoff *(left)* with one of
his clients, Meyer Lansky, in the 1940s.

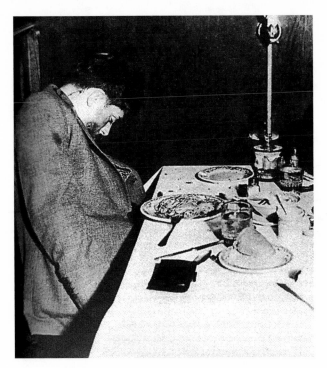

above

Joe "The Boss" Masseria shot dead
on April 15, 1931, in the Nuova Villa
Tammaro restaurant in Coney Island.
Lucky Luciano was in the toilet when
the execution occurred. He then
calmly called the police.

right

Joe Masseria's mug shot.

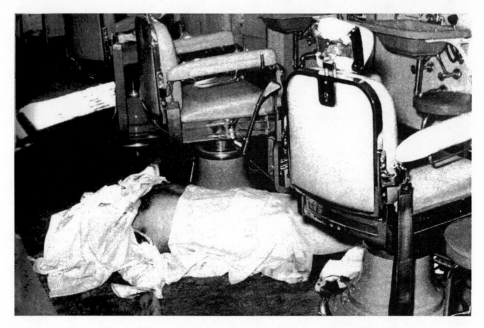

above
The October 25, 1957, murder of
Albert Anastasia in the barber
shop of the Park Sheraton Hotel
on Seventh Avenue and 55th
Street was decided the month
before at a Mafia summit at the
Hotel delle Palme in Palermo.

right
Albert Anastasia's mug shot.

left
Benjamin "Benny" or "Bugsy" Siegel.

below
Bugsy Siegel dead, June 20, 1947,
at the home of girlfriend Virginia Hill
in Los Angeles after mismanaging the
Las Vegas Flamingo Hotel venture.

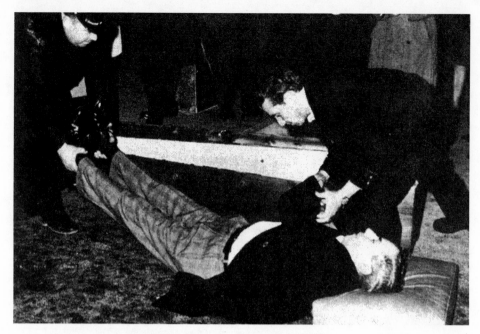

above

On January 26, 1962, Lucky Luciano died of a heart attack at Capodichino Airport in Naples while waiting for moviemaker Martin Gosch to arrive from London.

right

Luciano lived quietly in Naples for many years during the 1950s.

The main square in Gela a few days after the July 10, 1943, landings.

LA GRAN BRETAGNA HA FINALMENTE
SENTITO BEN PROFONDO NELLE SUE
CARNI IL MORSO DELLA LUPA DI ROMA

left
Civilians erase Fascist
propaganda off the
walls of private homes.

below
The desolation and
ruins of Palermo.

right
Mules for the U.S. Army
arriving in the port of Palermo.

below
The commander of the
Carabinieri reads an
Allied Military Government
proclamation to the
population. British AMGOT
officers are next to him.

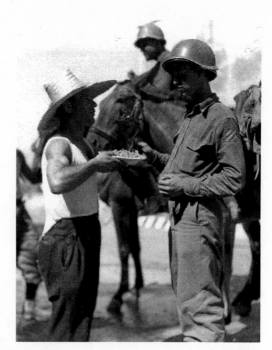

right
In Messina on August 14, 1943,
a peasant offers a plate of macaroni to
an American soldier.

below
A man sells melons by the pound.

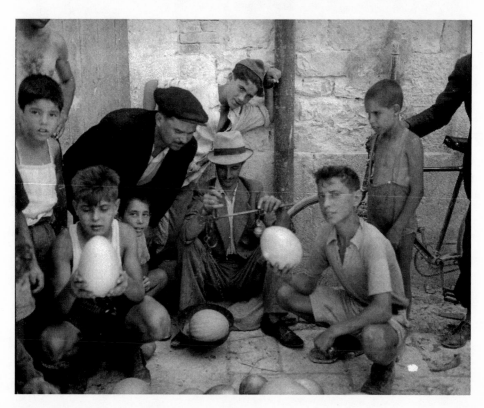

Chapter 4

Naval Intelligence Agents in Sicily

Immediately following the Casablanca Conference in January 1943, the ONI focused on Sicily. The idea of a direct attack across the English Channel into the heart of Europe massively defended by the Germans was definitely excluded. The landings in France were postponed for one more year. Following their victory in Africa the Allies were well positioned in the Mediterranean and had huge forces with which to attack Italy, Hitler's weaker European ally. The military might of the United States was obvious but the most unsettling intelligence was coming from Sicily, which included items such as: hundreds of Italian planes were ready to take off; the shaky allegiance to Fascism on the part of the soldiers stationed on the island; the strong anti-aircraft batteries disseminated throughout Sicily; the certainty that Sicilian soldiers would be among the first to surrender to the Americans. The Allies had to check this information to verify whether the Italian army would remain faithful to Benito Mussolini and how many were still ready to fight and die in order to defend Fascism.

The secret agents had very specific tasks: to contact friendly citizens and enlist their help in convincing the civilian population and the Italian soldiers to avoid fighting the Allies. This was not a simple mission; besides weakening the fighting spirit of Italian defenses it wanted to ensure that the Germans would be surrounded by a hostile population. Among the friendly civilians, according to Herlands, there were also many Mafia types from western Sicily. As Herlands noted, the Mafia leaders were looked up to in that part of the island in ways that Mussolini never dreamed were possible. Clearly the alliance between the U.S. Navy and the Mafia in far away New York would play a key role in the popular type of war that they sought in Sicily.

The ONI's Section F exclusively focused on Sicily. Section B-7 was under the command of Lt. Herman J. McCarthy. The first officer seeking information for B-7 was Lt. Joachim Titolo, who was a fluent Italian speaker and had worked closely with the district attorney. Titolo's mission was unique and consisted of gathering information from any source regarding Nazi and Fascist espionage operators sent by the German and Italian governments or by Americans who had embraced Nazism or Fascism. Such intelligence was very important since it allowed them to locate Italian industrial plants, port installations, beaches, coastal defenses, military installations and draw a picture of Italy's political and economic situation as well as the operations of German and Italian agents in the United States.

All this information was passed on to Haffenden, evaluated and sent through channels to the ONI in Washington. Haffenden was eager to obtain intelligence that would allow him to identify the locations and size of military and industrial installations. About one hundred of these items were generated through secret contacts in Sicily, with Italian army deserters and a few score civilians that included members of the Mafia.

Another officer working with Titolo was Lt. Anthony Marsloe, who was also fluent in Italian, Spanish, French, and the Sicilian dialect. Marsloe testified several times in front of the Herlands Commission and was one of the few witnesses who did not hide the ONI's purpose in reaching an agreement with organized crime and the support it provided to U.S. intelligence during the Sicilian campaign.

As Marsloe stated, B-7, just like the Intelligence Division, was involved in the unrelenting search for information of a strategic and logistical nature concerning the enemy and given his (Marsloe's) ability to speak the Sicilian dialects and his knowledge of Sicily, Commander Haffenden would send certain individuals whose names he did not even know or could remember. These people were first thoroughly questioned and then asked to provide photographs, documents, and other material of interest that were then sent to Cdr. Haffenden. It is possible that his deputy, Lt. Jamison, then filtered and analyzed the information. Later on a civilian named Tarbo used the documentation to outline possible plans that were then sent to the director of the ONI.

However, Marsloe mentioned no other names; he could not remember the names of the informers that were in the files, as he told the Herlands Commission, and could only say that Cdr. Haffenden on various occasions mentioned that there were many Italians and among them several named Luciano.

A few weeks before the landings Rear Admiral Henry K. Hewitt told his superiors that the planned creation of naval bases in areas recently liberated during the invasion could not proceed because it was impossible to establish close relations with the civilians in port cities in Sicily and particularly with the heads and members of the local Mafia. Thousands of tons of military supplies, weapons, tanks, jeeps, artillery pieces, and personnel were ready to be loaded on ships in the ports of North Africa for the invasion. However, there were no agents able to speak Italian and therefore capable of bringing back the necessary intelligence to set up the bases that had been planned for in enemy territory. Hewitt contacted the ONI directly in Washington, asking for six highly qualified officers to be sent over immediately. They had to be active and combat ready, having intelligence training and perfect knowledge of Italian. It was a delicate matter and Admiral Arthur Train passed it on to Commander Robert Thayer, who decided to use the Naval intelligence officers who were still working with organized crime in New York in the search for useful contacts in Sicily. Marsloe was one of these officers:

Thayer told me about a mission that would include handpicked personnel having excellent service records with experience in things Italian and who could speak the language. The mission was to land with the troops and handle certain key tasks.

Thayer picked two other officers who had participated in the Luciano operation: Lt. Joachim Titolo, who had assembled and analyzed a large amount of information about Sicily; and Lt. Paul A. Alfieri, an expert safe cracker and lock picker who had participated in secret searches of offices at the port of New York where spies were thought to operate. A third officer was Ensign James F. Murray, a young man who like the others could also speak perfect native Italian. The other two men were a German- and an Italian-language expert who were to stay in North Africa as back ups. The officers took a military plane out of Washington on May 15, 1943, flying over Newfoundland, Iceland, and the U-boat-infested North Atlantic, over Nazi-occupied Europe to finally land at Mers-el-Kebir in Algeria. The six navy men were sent to the Army Counter Intelligence Corps for intensive training in commando missions. They were then transferred to the French naval base at Bizerte, which had just been occupied, and reported to Rear Admiral Richard L. Connolly, in command of the forward bases and landing vessels. They were given their assignments for the landings in Sicily and their specific orders.

The mission comprised three main points: obtain information, immediately following the landings, from local inhabitants and Axis prisoners regarding the coastline and mine fields as well as the explosives for the destruction of the port installations; locate and take over as quickly as possible all existing documents at enemy naval head-quarters that had information useful to future operations; guarantee the security of the ports and organize counterintelligence operations at the forward naval bases. The four men had their own set of intelli-gence concerning the island from their contacts in New York with the Sicilian-Americans. Before leaving the officers and men had read through mounds of books, monographs, and assorted studies, including industrial research, to better understand the locations where they were supposed to land.

As Titolo remembered:

> The information I received from my sources gave me a clear picture of the topography of the Italian locations and in particular for some of them, besides the living habits, the political and economic situation of Italy and the islands; with other elements taken from many detailed descriptions of our objectives in Italy it became much easier for me to locate and take over the existing installations and immediately use the sources I needed to gather information. Before the invasion of Sicily, and as it was taking place, we got from the central offices of naval intelligence and from other sources of information complete and up-to-date publications with accurate information of the targets we were after. Each source of information was of vital importance to the others.

Lt. Alfieri described his impressions to the Herlands Commission about the days preceding his boarding a ship from Tunis to Sicily. He could see that over half the population of Tunis was made up of Italians of Sicilian descent. The areas subjected to the Allied blockade were all on the coastline but there was no doubt that ships, fishing trawlers, and small boats were able to maintain communications between Tunisia, Sicily, and the Italian mainland. The information that Alfieri had provided to the ONI Third District office in New York was vitally important during training in North Africa, as well as when the time came to prepare the operation itself. The information about the activities of the fishing boats and the type of informers on board was critically important, as well as the way they operated and the languages in which they communicated.

American and British secret agents were traveling from one North African port to another: from Casablanca to Tunis and to Alexandria in Egypt there was intense euphoria in the air at the end of June 1943. It was crucial that these agents to obtain information as well as disseminating disinformation about other potential landing areas. Titolo knew how small fishing boats traveling from North Africa to Sicily and the Italian boot also carried information across, and how most of the crews were actually engaged in smuggling contraband.

There was a tacit agreement between fishermen, smugglers, and secret agents. The fishermen would load up on cigarettes, flour, and other rare goods that could not be found in Sicily and convey them to the island. At the same time the ONI men used the fishing boats to reach a few coastal areas that were otherwise inaccessible. At times the little boats could not actually enter the port and the agents would only take pictures and make notes in their little notebooks. The OSS was also active in North Africa, along with the British, who were for the most part focused on the political situation in Italy and how to over-throw Mussolini and pry Italy out of the alliance with Hitler by offering an armistice with the Allies. The OSS was involved in the entire Italian territory rather than only with the conquest of Sicily. Therefore many OSS operations were not coordinated with other intelligence operations and Army headquarters. Its agents were more involved with operations and issues relating to postwar problems rather than research of information on enemy armaments or the loca-tions of mine fields.

Marine Colonel Angelo Cincotta, head of Section B-7I of ONI in Washington, arrived in Tunis. Haffenden had kept him in the dark about the agreement with Lucky Luciano. Cincotta did not mention Operation Underworld when he met with Titolo, Marsloe, and Alfieri even though all four officers were already in contact, as the Herlands Commission ascertained, with Mafia elements on the island and the colonel had seen the list the three young officers had of people they could contact in Sicily.

Marsloe and Murray, along with the men of the American unit called "Joss" that included General Truscott's Third Infantry Division and a Ranger battalion. The following day the soldiers landed on a front about twenty kilometers long between Torre di Gaffe and Punta due Rocche with their objectives being Licata and the Salso Valley. Two men reached Licata tagging along just behind a Ranger attack. Alfieri and Titolo landed in the Gulf of Gela with the *Dime* unit, which included General Allen's First Infantry Division and two Ranger brigades. Gela was occupied in the early hours that morning in spite of the harsh resistance of Italian soldiers that left 197 of them dead. On the same day two top U.S. intelligence officers landed in Sicily: the head of the OSS, General William J. Donovan, and another man who went by the code name of "Sorel" and was actually Michael Chinigo, a newspaper reporter for the International News Service. Immediately after they landed, as he was walking on the beach, Sorel heard the ring of a field telephone that had been abandoned by Italian soldiers. He lifted the receiver and heard a raspy and excited voice on the other end asking if in that sector of operations everything was all right: "We have a report that says the Americans have reached your sector..." "Absolutely not," answered Chinigo in flawless Italian. "Everything is quiet here. There isn't even the shadow of any American soldiers..." It seems that the clueless speaker was General Achille de Havet of the 206th Italian Coastal Division who fell for the deception and answered: "Keep your eyes open and signal any kind of movement."

A few years later Chinigo was awarded the Silver Star for his quick thinking. The four ONI officers immediately began collecting information from the civilians who were hiding in the caves in the countryside and in a few improvised shelters. Speaking in Sicilian dialect they were able to convince many people to come out of their hiding places, even though naval artillery was still firing at the coast. Many civilians collaborated by showing the location of mine fields along the coast and in the port areas. Many years later Marsloe agreed that the information was extremely valuable and helped spare thousands of men from death or mutilation.

Initial Contacts with the Mafia

Despite the overwhelming advance of Patton's troops the tough reaction of the Germans and the Italians at Gela forced the soldiers of the First Infantry Division to move back a few kilometers. While the battle for the town of Gela was in progress Marsloe, Murray, Alfieri, and Titolo decided the time had come to infiltrate behind enemy lines and contact the Sicilian Mafia.

Alfieri confirmed this to the Herlands Commission: one of the points in his mission was to contact Sicilians who had been deported from the United States back to their native Sicily because of criminal activities. After his arrival at Licata one of Marsloe's first achievements was to be able to contact many of these individuals. They were eager to help and were very useful, since they could speak English in addition to their own dialect.

To the question asked by Herlands—whether or not he could be sure that those Sicilians were part of the Mafia—Alfieri answered that they would certainly never have admitted as much. However, he could tell easily enough based on his experience with the investigations in New York. In any case most of these contacts were made possible through the cooperation of Lucky Luciano and the information received turned out to be very useful.

During the investigation some of the details of the work done in Sicily by ONI agents also came to light. Anthony Marsloe, the highest ranking officer of the group, confirmed the Alfieri statements regarding the collaboration of Mafia elements that added to the success of Operation Husky. The initiative of one member of the group who managed to penetrate behind enemy lines after locating the secret Italian naval command post made it possible.

That man was Paul Alfieri, who according to Marsloe's account, under a rain of artillery shells, mortar and machine gun fire managed to reach the enemy's front line and from there get to a magnificent villa on a little hill overlooking the sea. That villa, as they had learned in Africa and as the Mafia later confirmed, was the secret headquarters of the Italian navy located in a delightful country palazzo surrounded by palm trees, only a few hundred meters from the coast. When Alfieri entered the villa he discovered two Italian sailors looking at him in amazement and unable to muster of any kind of reaction. He walked right into one of the rooms where he found a small closet containing a safe. Even though he was an expert safe cracker he did not want to waste any time picking the lock, fearing that some Germans could suddenly appear. In front of the two silent Italian sailors he decided to blast the safe open rather than waste time picking the lock. He then grabbed the documents, waved at the two sailors, and fled back to the beach where Marsloe joined him. Together they made their way to the command ship where they reported to Admiral Connolly, who was amazed at the stack of documents they were delivering to him. There were encrypted German and Italian messages but the grand prize undoubtedly, and the documents that prompted Alfieri to go to the villa in the first place, were the order of battle and the locations of all German and Italian naval forces in the Mediterranean, the map of the minefields in the area, and the German overlays of the passageways within the mine fields.

Alfieri was awarded the Legion of Merit for his brave action with the following citation: "Thanks to his initiative and his courage that are part of his unique sense of duty he was able to provide extremely valuable information for the preparation of future operations, thereby contributing in large measure to the success of our invading forces."

While Alfieri's medal also went symbolically to all ONI personnel for an act of true heroism, it also officially recognized the existence of an agreement between the Mafia and American naval intelligence.

To keep a close but secret watch over ship movements in the Mediterranean, Titolo and Alfieri also controlled the activity of fishing boats operating off the southern coast of Sicily, using the recently acquired experience on the New York waterfront. As Alfieri explained in applying the techniques he had learned at the Third District Intelligence Division, he planned a similar operation for Sicily. The new organization was headed by Lt. Titolo and provided useful information to the navy in ferreting out suspicious naval movements. It is true that the first task of the Sicilian fishing fleet was to provide fish for the local population once the invasion was completed. But Lt. Titolo instructed the captains of the fishing boats to provide sensitive military information that turned out to be extremely important during the first difficult days of the invasion.

The contacts with the fishermen would have been useless without the help of local Mafia soldiers. Titolo confirmed this during his testimony to the Herlands Commission. Titolo's answer to the question whether he had established contact with the Mafia to reorganize the Sicilian fishing fleet was, "Yes we did and the information received was also very useful."

Chapter 5

The Corvo Plan and Operations in Sicily

Max Biagio Corvo was 22 years old when Earl Brennan appointed him to head the intelligence operations of the Office of Strategic Services in Sicily and later in Italy itself. His identity card carries number 45 and his code name was "Marat." In a very short time he went from the rank of private to being the lynchpin of the Italy Section of American intelligence. He became the officer within the OSS to plan methodically and in infinite detail the gathering of information to prepare for the political and military offensive against Mussolini's Fascist regime and specifically for the occupation of Sicily.

Max Corvo began drafting his plan in the spring of 1942 at the Quartermaster Training Center at Camp Lee, Virginia, where to his great disappointment he was assigned as a chaplain trainee. He was already thinking of a possible attack by American troops in Italy to bring down Mussolini's regime but he knew this could only happen with preliminary and very detailed intelligence planning and the careful recruitment of appropriate persons ready to work with Army intelligence. Corvo was highly motivated by anti-Fascist ideals that his father had instilled in him since childhood. Cesare Corvo was forced to immigrate to the United States from his hometown of Melilli in the province of Siracusa because of his opposition to the violence of Mussolini's black shirt squads. Another young man, who was his neighbor from Melilli, had lost his life during clashes between Fascists and Socialists and Corvo's house had been the target of machine gun fire by the black shirts. With the help of Don Luigi Sturzo—the Catholic priest and founder of the Democratic Partito Popolare, the future Christian Democratic Party—Cesare Corvo was able to leave Sicily and settle in Middletown, Connecticut. Max had been born three years before on October 12, 1920, and stayed behind in Sicily until the age of nine. He arrived in New York on the morning of October 12, 1929, just before the great Wall Street Crash. Both his origins and his father's reminiscences gave him a good knowledge of his country of origin and of the Sicilian mentality. All these factors led Corvo to write his own "Plan to overthrow the State in Sicily." These were a few ideas on ten typewritten pages describing the kind of operations that U.S. intelligence needed to engage in to undermine the Fascist regime in Sicily as a start and continue later on in Italy when an Allied invasion was contemplated. Corvo was transferred from Camp Lee to the public relations office at Camp S-2 while he was writing his plan. This transfer allowed him to complete the document and persuade some of his commanding officers to read it. On July 2, 1942, Corvo was called in to see Senator Danaher, who offered to explain the plan to Colonel Whelms, who was in charge of liaison with the Army for the Senate and later at the War Department. It did not take long for the paper to reach Earl Brennan.

As soon as Corvo entered the office of the head of the Italy section of the OSS he noticed a large map of Sicily hanging on the wall. On a table there were many Italian books. He discovered that Brennan was well informed about Italy and spoke excellent Italian. He didn't know about Brennan's past involvement in Italy as a diplomat and how he established connections with some elements in the leadership of OVRA (the Fascist regime's secret police) but also with the Vatican, the Freemasons, and many youthful followers of Mussolini.

Brennan was reading the eleven-page text entitled (in block letters) SICILY: HER ROLE IN THE MEDITERRANEAN CONFLICT. A PAPER ON THE SICILIAN PEOPLE AND THEIR ISLAND. At the bottom right-hand corner was the signature of Biagio, Max Corvo, Private Q.M.C., S-2 Section, Camp Lee, Va.

Brennan was clearly interested in the plan and asked Corvo to stay in Washington for six more days and do more research on anti-Fascist activity in New York that would be added to his report. Corvo agreed and found many more names and addresses during his trip. Upon his return Brennan placed him with other OSS agents working full time on what would be known later on as the "Corvo Plan." On August 5 orders transferring him from Camp Lee to Washington and the Strategic Service Training Unit came through. In the next few weeks Corvo took a course in paramilitary warfare for Special Operations (SO) in a location that is known today as Camp David. He also took a battery of psychological, endurance, and bravery tests perfected by the British. New OSS recruits from Norway, Hungary, Denmark, and Greece were also in training at the camp.

The Plan

"Italy is the Achilles heel of the Axis and Sicily Italy's weakest point. Should a second front be established this would be the most convenient location where we can succeed at the lowest cost." Corvo was probably the first American to share the same thoughts as Winston Churchill in the summer of 1942 while he was writing his plan about Sicily's role in the Mediterranean conflict. He was convinced that complete control of the area was a requirement to win the war and that any potential invasion of Sicily had to come from North Africa. But the conquest of Sicily had to include an understanding of the mentality of the Sicilian people.

As Corvo explained, Sicilians had been oppressed for many centuries and today Fascism is the newest oppressor. Sicily has provided the manpower for the many wars engaged in by the Fascists: Ethiopia, Spain, Albania, and North Africa, where thousands of young Sicilians died, many of them in horrible circumstances of thirst, hunger, and disease. The families got very little as reward. Sicilian soldiers were tired of continuous warfare and thought of their families who were being subjected to all kinds of shortages. They thought of the futility of the battles and their comrades who had died for nothing. They had nothing worth fighting for. The declaration of war on the United States created renewed feelings of despair and death. Few families on the island were without relatives in America, a country those simple people looked up to with respect as invincible, the land of opportunity and of plenty. Therefore war with the United States was something totally unthinkable for most people.

Corvo was convinced that a revolt was already brewing in Sicily and the gunpowder and detonators were ready. Someone had to set the fuse; the Americans had the means to do so but how could it happen in practical terms?

He wrote how propaganda and secret operatives could turn the situation around. The Sicilians were ready to rise up and rebel. Secret organizations did indeed exist but they had no assurances of obtaining outside help and that kind of guarantee must be provided to them, along with an effort to coordinate an attack from the outside and a revolt on the inside.

Corvo did not think that the Sicilians had to be subjugated nor were they "a lesser and backward civilization." Contrary to what the experts in the art of war believed, and Patton was certainly one of them, victory cannot be measured by the number of dead or the total weight of the bombs dropped on a city but in the actual ability of the winning side to act and get into the population's daily life by identifying its weaknesses and aspirations.

In his plan Corvo said that the prompting of the Sicilians to stage a revolt had to be undertaken by an organization that was fully aware of the people's strengths and weaknesses. Such an organization—and this was the novelty that drew Brennan's attention—had to include Italian patriots and most of all Sicilians who were ready to risk everything, including their own lives, to accomplish their mission. These persons would work directly with the anti-Fascist leadership living on the island, stirring up antagonism toward Mussolini and his ill-advised decision to go to war. It was also necessary to convince influential citizens of high rank within the Italian military with access to important information so that documents, maps, drawings of the mine fields and coastal batteries would end up in Allied hands and be used in military operations and the invasion of the island.

For the plan to succeed it was essential that the personnel for the mission be carefully selected. Corvo argued against the use of professional secret agents who would have stood out among the local population. The only people one could count on had to be true patriots coordinated by Italo-American agents with an excellent knowledge of Sicily. These true patriots were to organize small groups of trustworthy persons ready to engage in guerrilla operations behind enemy lines. Corvo felt that finding people he could count on would not be an issue since the average Sicilian is "enterprising and daring and loves to fight for a worthy cause."

The operational areas to be considered were those around the ports and military zones at Augusta, Catania, Siracusa, Messina, Palermo, Marsala, and Trapani. The eastern coast of the island was the more difficult one to clean up because it was heavily protected by mine fields and coastal artillery batteries. Those waters, however, were best suited to military operations and the plains near the sea offered the ideal terrain for landings and the movement of armored units. The guerrillas were to operate mainly inside the island where the primitive hilly landscape and damaged roadbeds made communications very difficult. The western part of the island, with the larger ports of Marsala and Trapani, was ideal for offensive operations.

The Recruitment

Max Corvo went to work in Washington recruiting the men who would be at his side to implement his plan. Even though British intelligence (SIS and SOE) were already trying to recruit Italian anti-Fascists for their Mediterranean operations and some New York anti-Fascist Italians were already enlisted in British intelligence, Corvo contacted some Sicilians who had worked with his father. Cesare Corvo had published an Italo-American weekly, *La Nave*, in Connecticut. Many anti-Fascists lived in New York while others had remained in

Sicily. Some of the letters they sent to Corvo, where they described the social and political situation on the island, were used in part as the preliminary intelligence material of the Italian Section of the OSS.

The first person Corvo contacted was Vincenzo Vacirca, an old acquaintance of his father Cesare, who had worked for the daily New York newspaper *Il Nuovo Mondo*. Vacirca had been a member of the Socialist Party and a deputy from Siracusa in the Italian parliament. He had moved to Switzerland once Fascism came to power and later to New York. In March 1926 Mussolini had revoked his Italian citizenship and confiscated all his property, accusing him of engaging in political activity against the Italian State and of criticizing Italy's international situation while in Switzerland and the United States. Vacirca was very sick with skin cancer when he met Corvo but still he agreed to discuss the situation in Italy. He also promised to assemble all the material he had on Sicily and mail it to him. Vacirca was the person who drafted the first appeals for psychological warfare targeting the Sicilian population.

The key men in the Italian Section of the OSS who worked in the front lines on Sicilian soil with Corvo were Vincent Scamporino and Victor Anfuso, both of them lawyers from Connecticut. Scamporino, also known as "Scamp," lived and worked in Middletown, a city that was home to many immigrants from Melilli and Augusta. He spoke excellent Italian and French and mostly handled labor cases. He was posted in Algiers as Brennan's representative. Brennan liked Scamp and the agents in Europe were ecstatic to be able to work with a man who spoke their language and understood their problems.

Victor Anfuso was from New York where he was known as a defense lawyer for many Italian immigrants. A Democratic Party regular, he had also been in contact with elements of the Mafia, including Frank Costello. Anfuso became Scamporino's deputy.

In that first group of volunteers, called "Earl's group" (after Earl Brennan), there were agents who spoke Sicilian and Sardinian dialects, like Frank Tarallo, who was also originally from Melilli and a Corvo family friend. He had played football at the University of Alabama, where he majored in foreign languages. Tarallo spoke the Sicilian dialect well and led the team that occupied the island of Ventotene, near Ischia, a mission for which he was awarded the Silver Star, the highest American decoration.

Other early recruits were Sebastian Passanisi, also a friend of Corvo's, who was about to leave for the Pacific when he called to join the OSS, and Louis Fiorilla, who had graduated from Wesleyan University in Middletown and had until 1937 studied to be a seminarian in Sicily. He was sent to take classes at the Radio and Cryptographic school. Then came another lawyer, Emilio Q. Daddario, known as "Mim," a football player at Wesleyan University who became Corvo's personal assistant; Joseph Bonfiglio, an officer whose parents were Sicilian; Nato De Angelis, who had studied drawing in Rome and Catania before the war and had volunteered to be a penetration agent; John Henderson, who had been a foreign service officer in Italy; Lester Houk had studied in Italy and was assigned as an analyst and writer; André Pacatte, who came from the Berlitz School in Cleveland and was chosen for his knowledge of Corsica; John Ricca, chief prosecutor at the municipal court in Detroit and who, during the war, would become a personal friend of Marshal Pietro Badoglio; Joseph Salerno, a staunch anti-Fascist and labor leader in Massachusetts, was one of the first recruits to attend classes at the OSS Training Center. And also Robert Marr from Cleveland, a transportation expert; Theodore Cutting, an army major and military liaison; Phil Adams, Albanian affairs administrator; Michael Chinigo, a reporter with the International News Service (INS); James Montante, a lawyer and Scamporino's executive officer; Joseph Russo, writer at the *Bridgeport Herald* and head of the Palermo OSS office after the occupation; Sal Principato, a labor leader from New Jersey; Egidio Clemente, a Chicago typographer; Umberto Galleani, who had been with the Loyalists during the Spanish Civil War; Joe Caputa, who was part of Tom Dewey's staff in New York, became a public affairs officer in Rome.

Among the first to have an OSS card there were also Alexander Cagiati, Dick Mazzarini, Pomp Orlando, Tony Ribarich, Luigi Di Maggio, Louis Timpanaro, Gaspare Salerno, Sam Fraulino, Giovanni De Montis, John Ballato, Peppino Puleo, and Vincent Pavia. These agents and OSS in general were very much maligned in the United States: what was held against them was their excessive freedom of action in operations and the large amounts of money that they handled with no oversight. For those who volunteered as civilians it was rumored that they were paid exaggerated salaries, as much as $250–$300 dollars a week—truly gigantic amounts in those days.

In a few months Corvo and his men contacted hundreds of persons of Italian origin living in the New York area. They were able to establish relationships with anti-Fascists who had fled Italy and in the United States were outspoken against Mussolini. Among this group there was the publisher Girolamo Valenti; Augusto Bellanca, a leader of the Amalgamated Clothing Workers of America; Luigi Antonini, an immigrant since 1908, a founding member of the anti-Fascist alliance, and president of the labor council and leader of the Liberal Party in New York State; Giuseppe Lupis, publisher of the monthly *Il Nuovo Mondo* and a careful planner in helping Corvo contact his Italian compatriots.

Corvo also had many meetings with Don Luigi Sturzo, the spiritual head of the anti-Fascist movement and who was living in Brooklyn after spending a long period in London. Sturzo had been threatened with assassination by the Fascists once he backed De Gasperi's position—Alcide De Gasperi was the Secretary of the Partito Popolare Italiano that Sturzo had founded in 1919—regarding collaboration with the Socialists. Sturzo fled from Italy on October 24, 1924, and lived in London until the end of 1940. He moved to the United States, where he remained until 1946. Sturzo's Italian connections and in particular his Sicilian origins (he was born and had lived in Caltagirone, a town in the province of Catania) were extremely useful to Corvo. Sturzo had created an association of democratic Italian Catholics called American People and Freedom and had strong ties to the Mazzini Society and in particular to Gaetano Salvemini and American academic circles. Corvo agreed with Sturzo's thinking about isolating Fascism from the Italian people. This drew Sturzo into a close relationship with the OSS, helping the cause by providing lists of trustworthy names useful for the landings on the island. Once he returned to Italy Sturzo reestablished his ties to his political protégés who were all destined to embark on successful political careers.

Corvo also contacted Colonel Randolfo Pacciardi, a tough man who had doctored his birth certificate at age sixteen in order to volunteer in the First World War. After the war the "little lawyer from Grosseto," as Mussolini referred to him, had founded Italia Libera, a political movement of anti-Fascist veterans. He was deported from Italy in 1926 after he defied Mussolini in public by marching in front of the famous balcony in Rome in protest. Pacciardi was among the first anti-Fascist militants to volunteer in the civil war in Spain in 1936 to fight Francisco Franco; his Garibaldi Battalion defeated Fascist troops at Guadalajara. Pacciardi was also strongly anti-Communist and was later accused of conspiring against the Italian Republic to physically eliminate the Communists. His OSS codename was "Waverly" because he lived on Waverly Place in Manhattan. Corvo asked him to contact some veteran fighters from the Spanish Civil War, including monarchists like Count Carlo Sforza, Alberto Cianca, Alberto Tarchiani, and others who had left Paris for New York once the Nazis occupied France. Many of these same people had already been contacted by British intelligence, which planned for Italy to remain a monarchy at the end of the war. The relationship between the OSS and British intelligence was not cordial since both organizations did not trust each other. A specific request by Earl Brennan to the British for assistance in the landing of agents in Sicily was never acted upon. London responded that it wished there to be no interference with its work and that assistance would be available only in case it was needed. Washington adopted the same policy and in the future all operational plans were to remain "top secret" even for the British allies.

One of Corvo's closest collaborators during the recruitment period of the OSS was Girolamo Valenti, who emigrated in 1911 and became a labor leader after founding *La Parola del Popolo*, the newspaper of the Italian Socialist Federation and the Socialist Party. During the Second World War Valenti ran a radio program in Italian, broadcasting out of New York, other American cities and to Italy. Corvo found out from Valenti how disorganized the anti-Fascist groups were in New York and how they had been approached by the British. Corvo offered him an exclusive relationship with the OSS to return democracy to Italy.

Valenti accepted as an anti-Bolshevik and anti-Fascist Socialist but he informed Corvo that he would also be anti-Communist just as his newspaper had been in the past.

Corvo worked with Valenti for several months, talking with labor leaders, academics, lawyers, looking for volunteers ready to risk their lives to defeat Fascism. This took place without omitting the main task of planning political action and future operations by creating a permanent staff and training recruits for missions specific to Italy, Sardinia, and Sicily.

The political planning for the invasion of Sicily and later of Italy was of prime importance to the Corvo Plan. Besides the military support for Operation Husky, the OSS was very sensitive about political and institutional problems in Italy post-Mussolini and in the Mediterranean after the war. The Soviet Union remained the ghost of the liberators and Corvo and his agents had to chase it away.

The Italian Section's recruitment of Italians into the OSS relied on expatriates, anti-Fascists, members of the workers movement, Socialists, intellectuals, who in one way or another had problems with the Fascist government or were not welcome to Mussolini. Communists and members of organized crime were kept out of these connections. Corvo had no plans and did not contact organized crime.

The decision to forbid any and all connections to anyone tied to criminal organizations came once OSS and Treasury Department agents suggested that Corvo meet with Lucky Luciano. The Boss at that time was at Dannemora State prison where he was offering his Sicilian contacts to the U.S. Government. Corvo told Brennan there was little to be gained with such a connection that could later become embarrassing. The Mafia had been practically wiped out by Mussolini even though many Mafiosi had managed to hold on to power in 1922.

A former Treasury Department officer known as Mr. White, who had been recruited by Earl Brennan, proposed that Max Corvo have a meeting with Luciano. White was in the process of arranging the meeting but it is almost certain that it never took place even though at the Herlands inquiry into the services of Luciano to the U.S. Navy someone mentioned two mysterious visits to Luciano in jail where the name of the visitor had never been revealed. Most probably that visitor was Earl Brennan. There is only one document drafted by the OSS one month before the invasion and establishing the conduct of operations that mentions the tasks and methods to be used in Sicily for intelligence operatives where it may be possible to use local criminal elements.

With time, given the long tradition of banditry—said the document—the harsh economic conditions and the presence on the island of persons with Mafia connections in the past one may create a guerrilla group that could become useful. These groups could be used at the discretion of the commanding officer to support invading units, create diversions, and give credibility to false attacks. They could also be used independently from the invasion to terrorize local bureaucrats and upset the island's defenses.

Corvo, on the other hand, always maintained that during his mission to Sicily. "I never had contacts with members of the Mafia either in the United States or during my stay in Sicily. The Mafia had nothing to do with the invasion of Sicily and I challenge anyone who says so to provide proof to the contrary."

Another often repeated scenario is that Corvo had infiltrated into Sicily a few months before the invasion to connect with Mafia elements. In Melilli, Corvo's birthplace, there are still some who remember him being there a few days before the invasion of the island. Witnesses say they saw and met him dressed in civilian clothes with the local priest in the church of San Sebastiano. But there is no tangible proof to back up any of these assertions. It is true that once Corvo landed in Sicily with the American Seventh Army on July 13, 1943, he hurried up to the town where he was born but this only happened after the landings. An official OSS document drafted on June 10, 1943, one month before the invasion states that there were no OSS agents on the island at that time and that operations by British intelligence that cost many lives had been suspended.

At the end of 1942 the Italian Section of the OSS was working full time in seeking information to set up a series of support operations for the army during the first days of the occupation. Corvo quickly understood that there was no program for the locations included in military operations. He therefore set up a special course focused on the history and geography of Sicily, a description of the Fascist administrative structure, the police, OVRA counterintelligence, and the Italian press. From books and documents in various libraries, including the rich collection of the Library of Congress, Corvo and his team were able to find the valuable information they needed. There were 18th century British Admiralty maps full of important details about the Sicilian coastline. There were maps of caves and local sea depth, plus geological studies about the erosion of the coast around the whole island. A scale model of Sicily was created in the OSS lab where landing locations, cities, and distances were adjusted every hour.

With the help of the Veteran's Administration Corvo managed to compile a list of First World War veterans who had returned to Italy and had been receiving their pensions up to December 1941 from the United States government. Corvo used the list to contact those veterans living in Italy.

In the final months of 1942, while the OSS SI (Secret Intelligence) division was building up the list of individuals who were ready to collaborate with the Corvo group, Earl Brennan was able to set up a sensational spy operation concerning the war in the Pacific. The plot was hatched in the Vatican around the Secretary of State Monsignor Giovanni Battista Montini, who later became Pope Paul VI. In his book about the OSS Richard Smith tells how Montini received a strategic map of Japan with the locations of all the military industrial facilities in the country from the Apostolic Nuncio in Tokyo. The map, of incalculable military intelligence value, reached Brennan by a strange circuitous route. The Vatican sent it to the Irish embassy in Rome and from there it reached Dublin. In the capital of the Republic of Ireland an Italian OSS agent Riccardo Mazzerini, took the secret document to London and from there it was sent to Washington D.C. American bombers were able to inflict huge losses on Japanese military industrial plants in the spring of 1943 as a result. The operation was code named the "Vessel Project" and was in effect the first tangible cooperation between the Holy See and American intelligence. In a series of secret OSS documents from 1944 the Vatican was considered, because of its official position of "sacred neutrality," a haven for Anglo-American intelligence. The secret activity benefited greatly from the cover provided by the American ambassador, Myron Taylor, who had been at that sensitive post since 1939.

The OSS Operational Plan

Following the Casablanca conference the Italian Section was concentrating on gathering intelligence on the areas located in the southwestern part of the island, which included the American military areas. The plans were called *Implementation Study for Special Military Plan for Psychological Warfare in Sicily.* Corvo handled the preliminary drafts for three sections of the OSS: Secret Intelligence (SI), Special Operations (SO), and Morale Operations (MO), a complex task that included a vast amount of preparatory services for espionage, such as the cross checking of contacts with leaders of underground political movements, the Freemasons, public officials, and religious leaders. The indecision that existed regarding the actual D-Day for Sicily slowed down the work of the OSS, which was able to identify the main military objectives: roads, railroad bridges, power plants, port installations and so forth. Corvo and his team also wrote several appeals to the civilian population that were disseminated as leaflets from airplanes.

Intelligence operations were specifically focused on the subversive actions of agents who were to take advantage of the weakness and vulnerability of Sicily: jamming radio signals, secret messages, the forging of documents, blackmail, corruption, and the use of superstitions and typical local beliefs. They were also to encourage the passive resistance of the Sicilians, their hostility to the Fascist regime, and their resentment and antagonism toward the Germans. The plan also called for the creation of an intelligence network made up of local elements for psychological warfare against the enemy. Already on the island were a large number of anti-Fascists, whom the OSS knew could be bribed since they were dependent upon British and American trade, which had disappeared for three years with disastrous economic consequences.

The victories in North Africa brought thousands of Italian prisoners into American POW camps. This led to the idea of recruiting volunteers who were to be deployed in the initial phase of the occupation of Sicily. The units would be placed under Pacciardi's command and were to land on beaches close to Gela or near Capo Passero to initiate incursions in the coastal areas just ahead of American troops. That plan, however, was not implemented. As Corvo remembered it Pacciardi, through the OSS, contacted some of his old legionnaires in North Africa. He discussed the idea at length with Vincent Scamporino, who was about to leave for Algiers, and provided letters of introduction for some of his trusted friends in Oran and Casablanca. The actual creation of an Italian Legion seemed simple but the White House and State Department, under pressure from the British, looked into the matter. Precious time was lost and Earl Brennan, who favored the idea of such a Legion, ended up shelving the plan. The idea was brought to the attention of General Marshall, who cabled General Eisenhower on June 23 to say that there was reluctance on the part of the State Department to give officer's rank to Pacciardi because he had fought with the Communists in Spain.

Following Max Corvo's suggestion, Brennan appointed Vincent Scamporino as Corvo's deputy, with full responsibility for the Italian Secret Intelligence section. Still in Washington and waiting to ship out to North Africa, Corvo continued his recruitment efforts. At that time he regularly patronized the Trianon restaurant, run by a man called Luigi, who was originally from Palermo. Located at Pennsylvania Avenue and 22nd Street, the Trianon was a favorite meeting place for OSS and State Department employees.

The First OSS Agents in Sicily

As soon as Scamporino reached Algiers Corvo began preparing to send his first agents into Sicily. The group included nine soldiers and two officers, both fluent in Sicilian and Sardinian dialects. The eleven men, under the command of Captain Frank Tarallo, were integrated into army units to facilitate their movements. Soldiers and weapons supplies were given top priority for transportation. Donovan signed the orders on March 13, 1943. On the next day "Earl's first group" was on board ship bound for Casablanca. From there they traveled by train through Morocco and Algeria until they reached the training camp called "Club des Pins" just outside Algiers, where they learned how to jump with a parachute, send cryptographic messages, send Morse code, read naval maps, march in muddy terrain for hours, and overcome various barriers and obstacles.

OSS headquarters was located in Algiers under G-3 of Allied Forces Headquarters in the magnificent Villa Magnol, where Colonel William Eddy worked with his small staff. At the end of April Eddy began pressuring Brennan so that his agents—another group had by then arrived at the training ground—could be involved in intelligence-gathering activities and justify their presence in Africa. That was how the head of the Italy Section at OSS appointed Max Corvo to travel to Algiers and set up military operations. After meeting with Donovan and with the rank of Second Lieutenant Corvo left for Algeria carrying two cases of documents he needed to prepare the final phase of operations. His travel orders were dated May 20, 1943, showing that his plane would be in hangar number 6 at Washington airport to depart at 9 a.m. The large TWA airliner that had been converted into a military transport took off for Algiers following a very circuitous route: after a stopover in Miami it went to Cuba, then to British Guyana and to Brazil. Over Dutch Guyana one engine stopped and the pilot had to land at the small airport at Paramaribo. An entire week was lost because of repairs and Corvo finally arrived in Algiers on May 28, where he was expected by Col. Eddy and Vincent Scamporino.

The islands of Pantelleria, Lampedusa, and Linosa were occupied by British troops on June 11 to 13. Over 6,000 tons of bombs were dropped on those smaller islands south of Sicily. For the Allies it was a dress rehearsal for the upcoming Operation Husky, which was why the preliminary bombings were codenamed "Workshop." The surrender of those small Mediterranean islands came with a very strong negative emotional impact on the Italian army and the population's morale. There were 11,000 Italian prisoners and many deaths among soldiers and civilians. The massive bombing also confirmed that the psychological war on the defenseless civilian population had also begun. It was a clear signal to Corvo and Scamporino that the invasion of Sicily was now at hand. Col. Eddy informed Scamporino that he needed a man who would be able to be his understudy in the secret operation on the island. This was the first time the OSS was getting ready for a military operation.

On July 8 Max Corvo and Capt. Frank Tarallo, under Col. Eddy's orders, joined up with the U.S. Seventh Army at the French naval base at Bizerte, ready to board ship for the Sicilian coast. They took a small amount of equipment along, such as radio transmitters, false documents, and civilian clothes. However, they were stopped by an officer as they were about to board because the date had changed to D-4, or July 14.

Corvo was disappointed because it meant that OSS operations would be delayed. He found it hard to believe that the OSS had not been informed of the actual plans for the troops. At dawn U.S. soldiers would land in Sicily and Operation Husky would begin.

Corvo and Tarallo found out at Bizerte that disaster had struck the 82nd Airborne. The plan called for a drop at midnight on July 9 of over 3,000 paratroopers under General James Gavin on certain strategic areas of the Sicilian coast. From bases in North Africa 266 C-47 transport planes had taken off but the very strong head winds over Sicily that night scattered most of the paratroopers. Many were killed by anti-aircraft fire and others landed on the roofs of houses. One group of 75 paratroopers even landed in far off Avola, which was within the British zone where General Kirkman's 50th British Army Division had no clue that there were any Americans in the area and opened fire, thinking they were the enemy. To be recognized the U.S. paratroopers had to put their helmets on their rifles and yell that they were not Italians. A British soldier told his commanding officer: "What in hell's name are those damn Yankees doing around here?"

On the afternoon of July 13 the three operatives went on board an LST along with Psychological Warfare Branch personnel in charge of disseminating information to the Italian newspapers and radio stations operating in Sicily. Among them was Colonel John Wittaker, the former *New York Times* correspondent in Rome before the war. Corvo, Tarallo, and Colonel Eddy were ashore around noon and immediately went to the Seventh Army headquarters.

As Corvo remembered it was broiling hot and all vehicles created a cloud of white dust permeating everything. Long columns of German and Italian prisoners were marching to the beach to board the ships that would take them to Tunisia and Algeria. That part of Sicily looked almost like an extension of North Africa, since the climate and vegetation were identical and there were no towns to speak of. Colonel Eddy was intent on finding a place to camp while there was still enough light. He had placed his cot and produced a bottle of Scotch, offering Corvo and Tarallo a drink, but they declined. Eddy, on the other hand, drank quite a bit in the next few hours.

The next day they proceeded to Licata where General Patton had set up his headquarters. On the way they saw the castle of Falconara, owned by the aristocratic Bordonaro family. It was a delightful place surrounded with palm trees and exotic plants with an old overseer the only tenant. From the castle there was a panoramic view of the coast of Sicily and Corvo could see the long dotted line of military ships continuing to unload men, weapons of all kinds, and other military supplies. He requisitioned the castle and made it OSS Operational HQ.

The meeting with Patton was far from friendly and the general let Col. Eddy know very clearly that he was not about to let anyone interfere with his race to Palermo. As Patton put it, intelligence operations were surely very useful but only when they did not waste time and interrupt the army's advance. Patton was not the only commander among the officers of the Seventh Army to have an aversion for the OSS; the traditional U.S. military intelligence G-2, CIC, and ONI felt the same way. The occupation of Sicily was the first exposure of Donovan's men to the need to coordinate their mission with military operations while the planning of Sicily was mostly a British affair. The OSS did not have an overseas section to produce documents. Their mission was mostly gathering tactical and strategic intelligence behind enemy lines and it required enlisting local people and working with them. In fact, the entire operation was seriously understaffed. There were really very few Italo-American volunteers who were capable of making war on their own relatives.

As Corvo states, deep infiltrations risked overtaking the vanguard units thus exposing the men to extreme danger without reaching any intelligence objectives. Local people were to be recruited for tactical missions to succeed. The data had to go by courier to the military unit needing it. These operational details should have been planned ahead of time and prior to the invasion. Had that happened, OSS units could have taken part in the initial phases of Operation Husky; many mistakes could have been avoided.

Corvo discussed the matter at length with General Donovan, who was back at Gela after his perilous landing on the first day of the invasion with Patton's men. At Falconara Castle the two OSS officers agreed that if the army continued its rapid advance the OSS infiltration operation would not have been useful. Corvo then asked Colonel Eddy for permission to go to the eastern coast of Sicily where he could make contact with some of his father's friends. The request was approved on July 16 and Corvo, now a captain, left for Siracusa, the province where he was originally from. With him went his driver, Carl Bommarito, and Serafin Buta, an expert radio operator who kept in contact with Falconara. In transit through Ragusa Corvo stopped in the main square in front of the church of San Giovanni where a large group of elders was assembled. Corvo inquired about Joe Lupis, who came from there, but none of the old men remembered him. He went on through small towns: Modica, Rosolini, Noto, Avola, and reached Melilli in the early hours the next day. He first met with Reverend Salvatore Fiorilla, the parish priest of the cathedral of San Sebastiano, with whom he discussed the very serious social situation that existed in the town and the possibility of finding persons willing to cooperate with the OSS. The city of Augusta was being repeatedly bombed, as well as Catania. From the high ground around Melilli at night came the sad spectacle of the sky lit up as though it were daylight. At Augusta Corvo was able to recruit one of his cousins, Pepé Catalano, who got busy looking for others willing to provide information about the German positions. Corvo's idea was to get behind enemy lines and obtain first-hand intelligence. He ordered three of his newly established teams to move along the road from Sortino to Vizzini and keep going to Caltagirone. The group left on the morning of July 18 with mules carrying bales of wheat. They were to move behind German lines, take mental notes of the military positions on the hills at the edge of Caltagirone, and report back to Corvo. When he returned to Falconara he was able to report to Col. Eddy that the mission was successful and they both left for

Caltanissetta, which been heavily bombed at that time and where they seized the archives of the prefecture. Among the documents was information about enemy positions in Sicily.

In the deserted streets Corvo could hear the moaning of victims caught under the rubble. In the panic during the bombing, the civil servants and the population had fled the city very quickly and no work teams had been organized. The dead bodies were covered with flies as they decomposed quickly under the broiling summer sun. The army had no time to help those unfortunate victims and Corvo finally had to go to a nearby POW camp for work teams.

At Caltanissetta Corvo arrested Colonel Pagano, an Italian officer who was in charge of food supplies for the area. After the interrogation Corvo ordered him to open the stores and distribute all the foodstuffs to the population: flour, wheat, salt, sugar, and other staples. Among the documents in his possession Corvo found how local gangsters had already benefited from the illegal food distribution.

Contact with OSS headquarters in Algiers was maintained through the small radio installed at the Falconara Castle. Ralph DeHaro, the radio expert, had sent messages about the progress Corvo and his newly activated groups were making to Vincent Scamporino. One message read: "The speed of the Sicilian campaign has made our plans redundant and infiltrations are almost impossible. Patton's troops are moving too fast for even our efficient intelligence techniques." Even so Donovan, who was still in Sicily, appreciated the intelligence work Corvo had undertaken until then with his small unit.

After Patton took Palermo on July 22, 1943, Corvo expanded his contacts to a few university professors to translate the many documents that had been seized. On July 25 the crowds filled the streets to cheer the news that Mussolini and Fascism had finally fallen.

Friction Between OSS and CIC

Palermo had been heavily bombed by the Allies and the areas around the port installations were reduced to rubble, while in the streets one felt the desperate struggle of the population to survive. Barter was a way of life for most people. American soldiers filled the city streets giving away cigarettes (even to children) and canned food to the prettiest girls in exchange for a smile. The Sicilian capital was the headquarters for the various intelligence agencies, including the CIC— Counter Intelligence Corps. There was antagonism between the CIC and OSS because the former was also gathering political intelligence, an area the OSS thought it should control exclusively. Despite the basic difference in the task of each agency (the OSS had the mission of restoring democracy and forcing Italy out of the war, while the CIC was in charge of preventing and punishing any threats to the well being of American soldiers), there was a keen rivalry between the two intelligence units, which at times created embarrassing problems. The CIC was a large centralized organization with the very specific goal of carrying out army counterintelligence that also included the recruitment and training of new men in support of military operations. Since January 1942 it had replaced the Corps of Intelligence Police, which had been originally set up by the War Department in 1917.

In Sicily the CIC's mission was to ensure the protection of U.S. personnel from possible reprisals or paramilitary actions that could originate with enemy spies, saboteurs, or Nazi and Fascist sympathizers. American soldiers were in a land they knew nothing about, surrounded by people who spoke a different language, and the locations could be extremely threatening. To avoid problems the army placed CIC agents within the units usually attached to a logistics company for food and accommodations. The unit commander was part of general headquarters and each CIC officer had his operating plan for the unit he was attached to. The overall plans were drafted for every province in Sicily and the target areas were set up in each city. Among the various tasks figured the inspection of landing areas, and the areas of operation to check the security situation. CIC teams were also trained for physical endurance and how to behave in case of capture. For Operation Husky a team of 16 officers and 76 agents were part of the divisions and infantry corps of the Seventh Army.

The operative CIC units were generally with the forward troops searching for information of vital importance to G-2, the army intelligence division. CIC agents took part in the occupation of Gela and Licata and later of Palermo. They often entered towns and villages ahead of the soldiers. When Axis troops retreated from Agrigento on July 17 seven CIC soldiers were in the city alone for five hours before Patton arrived. As they entered the city a frightened crowd was looting the shops and private houses and it was only with the assistance of the Carabinieri, the fire department, and a few priests that the CIC men were able to control the chaotic situation. They had also been trained to use force to prevent food riots that often took place before AMG units took over.

In November 1943 CIC agents captured a team of twenty-eight Fascist saboteurs in Trapani that according to a long CIC report had been financed by a wealthy woman. Two conspirators were arrested as they attempted to lay mines on a rail line in the outskirts of town. Other measures were adopted in the populated areas to control the municipal services, the Carabinieri, the police, the economy, the prisons, the headquarters, and personnel of political and military organizations. The Church was asked to help and after some high-level discussion with the military, civilian, and religious authorities a proclamation was issued laying down the rules of political behavior. From the end of July on CIC personnel were investigating in depth every large town within the Seventh Army sector.

The fast advance of the American army also created serious problems for CIC. Just as it happened to OSS men, CIC agents had to alter their plans several times because of the headstrong decisions made by General Patton and some of his officers. Counterintelligence units often reached the front lines after the troops had already left, creating confusion for those involved in operations and doubling the work the units had to perform. In Palermo as in other provincial capitals in western Sicily the CIC created a so-called "static-group," a unit dedicated to security problems in close contact with local Carabinieri and other such units. Informers were particularly well received and richly rewarded. Political intelligence was gathered within the CIC units where anyone "ready to cooperate" could walk in. The parish priests were the best sources in most cases. However, in occupied cities the CIC was being used mostly to reestablish order, secure documents, place fascist leaders under arrest, and investigate civilian employees. AMG personnel were then informed of the political situation in order to replace the individuals who had been arrested. A CIC report dated July 1943 states that some five hundred people had been arrested, including members of OVRA (Fascist secret police created in 1930 to fight all forms of dissent) and of the "Squadre d'Azione" (action squad), best known for its use of castor oil and beatings on anti-Fascist elements.

A special section known as Division CIC Section was in charge of all Fascist documents. Many CIC reports to G-2 were detailed descriptions of the roads beyond the front lines and information about enemy troop concentrations and their movements in the territory, the morale of Italian and German soldiers, the location of minefields and road-blocks. There were also copies of the of battle order of enemy units operating on the island and the complete files on all prisoners in Sicily and Italy. CIC agents collected most of this material after Axis troops left it behind during their retreat.

Despite the hostility that existed between the Italy Section of OSS and the CIC, there were times when they worked together. One of the CIC's biggest problems was that they had few Italian speakers, while Corvo's men not only spoke fluently but also knew the Sicilian dialect very well. In some cases CIC officers had hired local civilians and at other times OSS personnel acted as interpreters.

The work done by CIC was in any case very useful in the period preceding the new organization of the Allied Military Government and many CIC areas were then transferred to the AMG. This happened due to the ambiguous and fine line dividing the responsibility of Military Police, local military commanders, and CIC; in many cases a liaison was required between the AMG and the CIC.

OSS Missions on the Battlefronts

Once Vincent Scamporino reached Palermo Max Corvo was able to spend more time at the front where he could see intelligence-gathering problems at close range and establish personal contacts with Seventh Army officers. It was a very fruitful time for intelligence collection on Axis military activity, not just in Sicily but also on the Italian mainland, Corsica, southern France, and the Balkans. Much of the information was about Italian commanding generals, the Italian army, and the geographic underpinnings of military troop movements. Those reports were full of details about the enemy's morale, the loyalty to Fascist policies or to the King, and the general condition of weapons and equipment. Most of the information was obtained thanks to the collaboration of an anti-Fascist lieutenant colonel of the Italian army who had been in command of a coastal battalion at Cefalù and whom Corvo had taken prisoner during his reconnaissance of the battlefront. The colonel had a file of eight pages giving a very detailed analysis of the allied invasion of Sicily. It was in fact a SIM (Servizio Informazioni Militare) report that provided, several months before D-Day, the dates of the landings and the units that were to take part in the operation. Such a well-prepared and detailed report came as a complete surprise to Corvo and the officers at Allied headquarters.

Failed Missions

In the chaotic Palermo of the summer of 1943 Lt. Col. Guido Pantaleoni arrived one morning from North Africa. He was a New York lawyer and an officer of the Special Operations Branch of the OSS. His men were trained to create chaos and disorganization within enemy ranks and to damage its morale. In his pocket he carried orders to lead a team of agents and soldiers on a mission into French territory. During the first days of August, while the Germans were retreating to Messina, Max Corvo thought it necessary to have his agents land on the Tyrrhenian part of the Mediterranean front, near Cerami and Capizzi, north of Troina. The American advance toward the Straits of Messina had been slowed down considerably and the movement of the men of General Middleton's 45th Division along the coast was extremely slow, both because of the shelling from Italo-German units and the destruction of the roads by Axis engineers as they were retreating. The 1st Division was engaged in a tough battle at Troina against a diehard group of Germans holding on to excellent positions around that town astride a high mountain pass. There was no good news coming from that part of Sicily to Corvo, who wanted to dispatch some of his men to check the information regarding enemy fortifications and German resistance capabilities. Colonel Pantaleoni volunteered to lead the unit, telling Corvo that it would provide him with necessary experience for his mission to France. Corvo agreed, giving him four men and the orders for the mission that was to have tragic results.

Once he left Palermo, Pantaleoni and his men took the road to Nicosia, where they bought some mules to go on to Capizzi in the Nebrodi mountains. They reached the command post of the 1st U.S. Division, which was then was engaged in battle against the Germans. Private Anthony Ribarich, one of Pantaleoni's men, gave a very detailed account of the mission in the report he wrote upon returning to Palermo:

On Friday, August 6, we went to Monte Battaglia and without any problems continued toward Monte Finocchio, where we spent the night. On Saturday morning, after asking several local peasants who were knowledgeable of the area to guide us, we put on civilian clothes over our uniforms. We began crossing enemy lines at Acquarosa (the Passo dei Tre) and to make ourselves less conspicuous we decided to break up in three sections.

The first group included Tregua, De Angelis, and a guide with a mule carrying parts of the radio and forty-five minutes ahead of the second group; the second group with Buta and Ribarich and a mule carrying the other pieces of the radio with another guide; the third group with two civilians and two mules stayed behind in Acquarosa to wait for the return of the first guide. After a half hour's walk on the path we ran into an Italian army sergeant going in the same direction we were taking. He asked permission to place his rifle and backpack on the mule and I said yes. As we went ahead I understood the danger we would be in if we continued with the sergeant. I persuaded the Colonel and Buta to slow down and keep a distance. Once we came within three hundred meters of a bend we disappeared into the forest but we lost sight of the sergeant and the guide. The Colonel asked me to go back to find them since I was the only one to speak Italian. I turned back but after about one hundred meters I hit a mine. Fortunately I was only wounded in the neck. It was about 10 a.m. and after being helped by the Colonel and Buta we continued our march forward. We then hid on a side road to wait for the others who had left after us.

After some two hours I saw a German patrol guided by a civilian—he had also been seen by the third group of our mission. I barely had time to alert the others when the enemy saw us and opened fire. Given the situation we decided to take off our civilian clothes. I opened fire with my pistol and the others were also firing. The exchange of gunfire lasted some twenty minutes and the Germans had rifles and hand grenades. Buta was wounded in the spine and the Colonel in a leg. Once we saw that it would be useless to keep on fighting the Colonel decided to surrender. I disobeyed the order and despite being wounded several times I rolled down the hill chewing up parts of the documents I had on me. As I ran I detonated another land mine and last heard the Colonel say to the enemy that his group included Sergeant Buta and "Sergeant" Ribarich, thus promoting me on the battlefield. I barely was able to hide our civilian clothes and money. After about one hour as I was surrounded by enemy troops and had no possibility of escape, I surrendered. They took me to Acquarosa where I saw Buta on a gurney. I couldn't find the Colonel, who was removed immediately following his capture. The two peasants who owned the land and whom we befriended were also captured and later killed.

In his long report dated August 13 Private Ribarich also mentioned his dramatic escape after being taken to a camp of the 15th Panzer Regiment.

They told me to get in car with a German lieutenant. Some retreating soldiers were setting mines on the road and around the trees on either side. We went to Randazzo, stopping several times. On Sunday morning the German lieutenant ordered a guide to go ahead and make sure we could move forward. I was alone with the German, who after a few minutes fell asleep in the car. I took out a short knife I had hidden and in one sweep slit his throat. I ran very quickly and got lost in the forest. At dawn I found a farmhouse and approached it carefully. Some peasants welcomed me and offered food and civilian clothes. After a few hours I walked to our positions near the village of Cesarò.

Corvo found out about the failure of the mission a few days later once Private Ribarich was taken back to Palermo and could tell his story. He considered another mission to save Colonel Pantaleoni by sending a few men back to the front, among them the same De Angelis and Tregua. The OSS team left the next day but found no trace of Colonel Pantaleoni. Other attempts also proved to be futile, and Red Cross inquiries never located the officer.

During the brief Sicilian campaign there were few operations on the island itself. Corvo and his men spent much of their time trying to figure out how the gathering of intelligence was slowed down by the absence of a support group that would guarantee the agents a minimum possibility of success and would not waste the human resources that the Italy Section of SI was so proud of. There were too many layers between the army and the OSS. The failure to provide support and cover during the transfers of documents and information was a crippling form of disorganization. Very few agents trained in the camps in North Africa were able to reach Corvo in Sicily at that time. The careful and thorough recruitment effort that had started in mid-1942 seemed useless given the results achieved until then. At the beginning of August, not a single operational group that had been trained in the U.S. was able to reach Algiers. Only two officers made it to Africa: Colonel Russ Livermore and Lt. James Russo, but they were being trained for future operations inside Italy.

The OSS leadership, instead of consolidating operations in Sicily, was in fact creating a new command structure for the invasion of Italy. In a report dated August 25, 1943, Colonel Rudy Winnacker, who had opened the first office of the OSS Research and Analysis Branch (R&A) in Palermo, stated that the work had to be undertaken despite the innumerable problems that existed with G-2 and other intelligence units, using local personnel very carefully to avoid any serious breakdowns. I have worked with my interpreter Charles Moia of the

Italian section and have used some old Italian agents who have not been trained to do this type of work."

On August 14 Corvo planned operations to land a few OSS men on Italy proper. After a meeting with some officers of Army G-2 he proposed a preliminary operation to occupy the Aeolian Islands (in the Tyrrhenian Sea), which were penal colonies defended by a few Italian naval and army units. The penitentiary at Lipari, besides common criminals, also included political dissidents and anti-Fascists. The operation was not supposed to result in bloodshed and therefore required a way to get close to the coast without raising the alarm. The men who took part in the mission were Capt. Frank Tarallo, Lt. Henry Ringling North, and Pfcs. Louis Fiorilla, Benny Treglia, Peter Durante Egidio Clemente, John Ballato, Carl Bommarito, Nato De Angelis, and Barney Tumbiolo, and AMG Capt. Camby. Capt. Tarallo was in command. The group left on several boats escorted by a U.S. destroyer ready to step in in case they encountered enemy fire. The boats drew close to the small port of Lipari, guarded by Italian soldiers. Capt. Tarallo and two men swam ashore. Out of a shelter behind the port's jetty an Italian officer emerged carrying a sword and a piece of white cloth. The conquest of the island was a very simple matter.

The Corvo team confiscated weapons, ammunition, and documents and freed the prisoners. Tarallo questioned forty-five prisoners, including two anti-Fascists who had been locked up for two years. In the end the islands and their population of eight thousand were administered by the AMG.

Corvo was personally involved on the island of Favignana just off the edge of eastern Sicily. Like Lipari, Favignana also had a penitentiary that housed common criminals and political prisoners. There were some Mafia individuals who had been sentenced by Fascist judges. When Corvo opened the gates and freed the prisoners, the Mafiosi were also set free.

As Corvo recalled, all political prisoners were released. But he did not release anyone who had been condemned for committing a crime. The Mafiosi were in jail for criminal acts and they did not interfere with the OSS. Obviously once the islands were liberated they found ways to return to Sicily or the Italian mainland.

Chapter 6

The Americans Arrive

To the anonymous American combat cameraman the old gentleman in a corduroy jacket, white shirt and tie and, a grey cap on board a U.S. Navy ship in July in the Bay of Gela must have looked strange enough. He saw him arriving in a small boat with two very solicitous soldiers who helped him up the ladder then down again to return to shore. That civilian being given the royal treatment by his superiors prompted the cameraman to roll the film for a few seconds and the images open the question of who was coming and going on U.S. Navy ships. Who was the older man in those old film clips? His identity remains unknown. Yet the cap, the jacket and tie all take on a special meaning in the unwritten communications used by Sicilians. He was certainly no peasant, or bureaucrat, fisherman, or spy. One may say that he was simply a man who commands respect, dressed that way, and that he was treated as such since he was being ushered on board the ship acting as ambassador for another even more important

man who commanded much greater respect. He was just one of the
Mafiosi whom ONI agents Marsloe, Murray, Alfieri, and Titolo mentioned in their testimony to the Herlands Commission and that they
had used "in order to avoid wasting the lives of many young American
soldiers." To prevent any strife with the civilian population during the
occupation of the island. He was on that ship to provide information
about what was happening on the Italo-German side of the front
where many units were already getting ready to retreat to the high
ground of the Madonie on their way to Messina and then Calabria. He
had gone there probably to confirm that the signal from the American
"friends" had reached Sicily and that someone had already given to
Mafia leader Calogero Vizzini the yellow scarf with a black "L" em-
broidered on it sent by Lucky Luciano as the symbol of cooperation
between the Mafia and U.S. intelligence.

The story of that yellow "flag," that many think of as a legend, can
be found only in the memory of those who lived through it, since no
other document about it exists. Michele Pantaleone, a fellow citizen of
Don Calò Vizzini and a Socialist Party leader who spent most of his
life writing against the Mafia and denouncing its massive presence
within various political parties, told what happened during those sad
days of 1943 when the relationship between the Mafia and U.S. intelligence was cemented in Sicily:

> On the morning of July 14 an American fighter plane appeared
> above Villalba. The plane flew so low as to almost touch the roofs
> of the houses and then one could see the strange sign floating on
> the fuselage: a gold colored cloth with a giant black "L" in the
> center. At one point, near the house of Monsignor Giovanni
> Vizzini, the parish priest and brother of Don Calò, the plane
> dropped an envelope containing a scarf identical to the cloth
> flapping from the plane. The scarf was found by a soldier, Raniero
> Nuzzolese da Bari, who quickly handed it to the local Carabiniere,
> Angelo Riccioli from Palermo, then stationed at Villalba. The next
> day the plane returned with the same cloth and dropped a second
> bag on the village of Gozzo di Garbo, right in front of the Vizzini
> home. This time the bag, addressed to "zu Calò," was found by

Carmelo Bartolomeo a servant at the Vizzini house and handed
over to the addressee.

Bartolomeo later recalled the episode: "The scarf had an envelope
stitched to it and inside there was a smaller silk scarf looking like it was
made of gold with the same markings that were on the plane." Late
that night a peasant, nicknamed "Mangiapane," left Villalba on horse-
back to go to Mussomeli with a handwritten note from Don Calò
Vizzini for Giuseppe Genco Russo, also a man of honor at Mussomeli.
In typical Mafia language Don Calò was telling Genco Russo that on
the 20th a big shot at Polizzi Generosa, named Turi, was to accompany
the motorized divisions to Cerda while he, Vizzini, would leave on the
same day with the troops, the tanks, and the top commander. The
friends were to prepare the places to stop and bivouac for the troops.
The next day Mangiapane returned with Genco Russo's reply confirming to Don Calò that everything would be ready.

The Americans reached Villalba, the afternoon of July 20, 1943. All
morning, along the Salso Inferiore River, the Americans had been
doing battle with an Italian company that was successful in slowing
their advance toward the village. A jeep with an American officer and a
corporal went to Don Calò's house. Pantaleone wrote:

The car had a big yellow and gold flag with the black "L" in the
middle. But at the crossroad outside the village the driver had an
accident and the jeep went into the Lumera section where it was
fired upon by a rearguard of Italian troops commanded by Lt.
Luigi Mangano. One of the Americans was hit under the arm and
rolled on to the pavement while the jeep turned around suddenly
and went in the opposite direction. Later, a man from the village,
Carmine Palermo, went up to the American and seeing he was
dead took a leather bag where he found a letter addressed to Don
Calogero Vizzini, who received it immediately. Three large U.S.
tanks moved up to the village of Villalba the same day. One of
them had the big yellow-and-gold flag with the black "L" and an
officer speaking in a Sicilian-American accent asked for Don
Calogero Vizzini. Don Calò soon appeared in his shirtsleeves with

his jacket folded on his arm, a cigar in his mouth, and wearing a hat over his big eyeglasses. He moved slowly through the crowd as he always did, as though he were uncomfortable in his oversize body. Without saying a word he extracted a yellow handkerchief from his pocket showed it to the American and went aboard the tank with his nephew Damiano Lumia, who had recently returned from America. Before leaving he called Mangiapane and told him to go back to Mussomeli and tell "zu Peppi" what had happened in Villalba.

The village of Mussomeli had a few anti-aircraft guns and there were still many Italian soldiers on the surrounding hills on Monte San Vito, Palizello, and Cammarata from where they controlled a few important roads. To take Mussomeli the Americans would have had to fight and possibly suffer many casualties. On the morning of July 21 over half of the Italian soldiers didn't show up for roll call after being encouraged during the night by "some important friends to abandon their positions to avoid useless bloodshed." To those soldiers who dropped their weapons spontaneously the "friends" offered civilian clothes for them to return to their families. A column of American soldiers stopped for several hours just a few kilometers away from the village waiting for the signal to move forward from a stranger who just before had met with the Mafia leaders of Mussomeli in a farmhouse in Mintina. It was there that Giuseppe Genco Russo had captured infantry Colonel Giuseppe Salemi and "after disarming him had locked him up for three days in the social club at Mussomeli under the watchful guard of a few "picciotti." Russo was a kind of Mafia partisan who without firing a shot had managed to spare his area the rain of bombs the Americans would have dropped had they not been given the signal that the way was clear.

Similar episodes took place within the territory controlled by Don Calò Vizzini at Vallelunga: Salvatore Malta demanded the surrender of the Italian patrol, led by Lt. Luigi Mangano, stationed at Passo di Cunicchieddi in the village of Lumera; at Villalba Lt. Pilato was drawn into a trap in a warehouse owned by Vizzini. He was stripped of his clothes, disarmed, and held barefoot for two days so he couldn't communicate with anyone.

That yellow handkerchief therefore had a special meaning: it was a password for the Sicilian Mafia that the time had come to take sides with the Allies. It was the signal that Don Calò was expecting to welcome the American cousins.

A rather incredible story was told about the yellow handkerchief: in 1922 a man called Lollò di Villalba was caught committing murder and condemned to life in prison. Later he was said to be crazy and sent to the penitentiary for the criminally insane at Barcellona Pozzo di Gotto, near Messina. One night Lollò died. The body was placed in a casket that was filled with tiny flowers. He got out of the prison and out of the casket, which was buried empty. In the meantime:

> His friends had prepared so that he could secretly go to America and Don Calogero Vizzini gave him an elegant yellow scarf with a "C" embroidered in black in the middle, the initial standing for his first name and a sign for the friends who were expecting him on the other side of the Atlantic. Lollò used the scarf and was given a warm welcome by the families in New York.

At Villalba Don Calò Vizzini climbed aboard a U.S. tank that then drove away. No one ever found out where he went. He came back six days later. On July 27, 1943, in the Carabinieri's barracks, Lt. Beher of the AMG, under orders from Colonel Charles Poletti, appointed Calogero Vizzini mayor of the town. It was an unusually noisy ceremony with many people present. Michele Pantaleone was also there and remembered how things went that morning:

> A few nonresidents were also present at Villalba, including Dr. Calogero Volpe from Montedoro and Father Piccillo from the archdiocese of Caltanissetta, who paid a visit to Don Calò's brothers, who were also priests, as if to underline the close ties the Vizzini family had with the Catholic Church. Another group of close and trustworthy friends of Don Calò were outside the barracks and with boundless enthusiasm they were screaming

"Long live the Mafia! Long live crime! Long live Don Calò!" I made the mistake of expressing my contrary opinion to Don Salvatore Vizzini, Don Calò's brother and himself a priest—to whom I said that those words were shameful and offended the mayor's office. "Let them yell all they want," answered Father Salvatore. "It can help stop those who would otherwise prevent the appointment." And in an aggressive tone he asked, "What do *you* think about it?" I didn't say whether I approved of the appointment or the demonstration.

Immediately following the ceremony the new mayor had a meeting with his friends at his home, a group that also included a few American Civil Affairs officers. On that occasion the commander of the Carabinieri at Villalba, Pietro Purpi, following orders from Lt. Beher, allowed a few of Don Calò's men "to be armed with rifles, pistols, and revolvers to ward off any possible attacks from Fascists and carry out the tasks they were given by Mayor Calogero Vizzini and also help the Royal Carabinieri." An official declaration therefore allowed Don Calò to have bodyguards, most of them with criminal records. Soon after the commander of the Carabinieri was shot dead in the town's main square. The reasons behind Purpi's murder had a very precise origin: on the day Vizzini was elected mayor, Purpi had openly deplored the fact that Don Calò's men had yelled "Long live the Mafia." He had called in three of Vizzini's men to the barracks, Lupo, Spera, and Capitano, to whom he said he would put the facts on record in his official log. A few days later the commander was to be "slapped in the face by Giuseppe Scarlata, Lumia's brother-in-law and forced to take the affront without any reaction. He was shot in February 1944 as he entered the former social club that had become the headquarters of the Movement of Sicilian Separatists." The murder would remain un-solved.

With his appointment and clean bill of health as an anti-Fascist mayor by the Allied forces, Don Calogero Vizzini went right back to his unlawful activities. Revered and respected even more, Don Calò received many gifts. The U.S. command at Caltanissetta offered two trucks and a tractor to clear the rubble caused by the various bombings. Don Calò used the trucks to deliver foodstuffs destined for the black market. The town of Mussomeli sent the new mayor 50,000 lire that had been collected by his "friends." "The prefect of Caltanissetta, Arcangelo Cammarata, sent many pairs of shoes stolen from Italian military supply depots, showing how Don Calò's influence extended far beyond the territorial limits of Villalba." In those days the black market was a sure way to get rich. The control of foodstuffs and their distribution to the population had wound up in the hands of the Mafia. Some crooks were inside the public administration offices where they controlled the movement of goods and transportation. Just before the landings in many Sicilian towns there were several attacks on military stores that had been left unguarded by the soldiers during the retreat. At Villalba, Lercara Friddi, and Roccapalumba some Mafiosi got rich by selling stolen goods. Some 80,000 pairs of shoes were stolen from a railroad warehouse and sold on the black market during the following winter. At Villalba the population and the Mafiosi looted a warehouse filled with pharmaceutical products. Years later a marshal of the Carabinieri from Gela found a stolen truck in one of Calogero Vizzini's farmhouses that was used to transport stolen goods out of the warehouses. The main traffic in stolen goods, foodstuffs, and anything that was of vital importance to the population at the time was controlled by Vito Genovese, a gangster who worked with Lucky Luciano and had returned to Italy in 1937 to avoid arrest on a murder charge in Brooklyn. Genovese was given a warm welcome by the Fascist regime and its leadership for which he had organized many parties with beautiful women, cocaine, and excellent champagne. With the drug money (he kept 2 million dollars in a Swiss bank account) he had also financed the construction of the Fascist Party headquarters in Nola, his hometown near Naples. Genovese had also, several times, been a guest of the Duce's daughter Edda Ciano and her husband Count Galeazzo Ciano. In January 1943, to further ingratiate himself with Mussolini, he arranged for the murder in New York of Carlo Tresca, a personal enemy of Mussolini and the editor of the anti-Fascist newspaper *Il Martello* (The Hammer). Young Carmine Galante waited for Tresca at Fifth Avenue and 15th Street in Manhattan and shot him several times with a .38 revolver.

Vito Genovese was also able to insinuate himself into the AMG and secure a job as guide and interpreter for Col. Charles Poletti during the meetings held with public administration personnel. A close relationship existed between Genovese and Poletti and the Italo-American gangster gave the head of Civil Affairs at the AMG a luxurious 1938 Packard sedan as a gift. Genovese worked for the Allied command at Nola where he managed to establish contact with Calogero Vizzini. The two men set up an arrangement for the illegal traffic of foodstuffs: entire railroad cars filled with tons of pasta made at the mill at "Maria Santissima dei Miracoli" in Mussomeli, owned by Giuseppe Genco Russo, would leave Villalba regularly. In addition more trucks and trains full with flour, salt, oil, vegetables, and wheat would also be shipped to Nola. The precious cargo, shipped with legitimate documents for transportation approved by the AMG, also employed some of Don Calò soldiers. Once the merchandise reached its destination Genovese would take over and resell it on the black market. As Pantaleone would write about the summer of 1944:

> The Naples rackets police seized a railroad car near the station at Nola that was filled with lentils and beans from Villalba. Among the 300 sacks of 50 kilos each of vegetables sixty were filled with salt instead. The investigation concluded that the railroad car had been shipped at Villalba by someone using a false name and the name of the person receiving the goods did not exist both in Nola and in Sicily. There was heavy smuggling at that time from Sicily to the north with all the problems created by the destruction of transportation and communication lines, including the roads and railways by both U.S. bombing raids and German artillery. The rackets police in Naples asked the Italian treasury office in Caltanissetta to open an investigation at the Villalba railroad station. The job went to an older commander and a young officer known for having successfully solved many smuggling cases between Africa and Gela. The young officer, disguised as a "deal-maker," traveled to Villalba and after a series of problems managed to meet a broker called "Paesanello," who said that he had been the go-between in the purchase of lentils; from him it was simple enough to trace back to

those who had transported the cargo to the railroad station, loaded them on the train—all of them very close to Calò Vizzini. But the officer's work was destined to encounter massive obstacles. An order came from the Allied command in Palermo to close the file, since both the vegetables and the salt had been ordered by the military command.

In August 1944 Vito Genovese was arrested by FBI Agent Orange Dickey, who escorted him personally from Italy to a jail in the United States. Genovese was still wanted for the murder of a restaurant manager. Two gangsters were ready to testify—Peter La Tampa and Ernest Rupolo. Just before the trial La Tampa died of poisoning in his cell by swallowing an overdose of medicine for kidney stones. The Rupolo testimony by itself was not enough, since two eyewitnesses were required. Genovese was freed from jail on June 11, 1946.

During the period of the Anglo-American occupation of Sicily the Mafia worked hard to catch up after the years of persecution under Fascism. For Calogero Vizzini, Giuseppe Genco Russo, and others, however, it was essential to seek legitimacy for their power, which is why they agreed to accept Allied help, come out into the open, and shed their clandestine ways. As Pantaleone wrote:

> Mafia leaders were suddenly offered the opportunity to achieve status and business connections at the national and international level. The Mafia had prospered until then through alliances and political protection; it had become a social force of its own that could identify with political, military, and government power. Don Calò and many other big shots knew very well that sooner or later the golden AMG regime would disappear and it tried to find the political movement within the existing confusion that could allow them to benefit from the political situation and perhaps even orient its future course.

In the beautiful villas of Mondello or the Conca d'Oro, in the turn of the century palaces of Palermo (slowly recovering from the brutal bombings of 1943), Colonel Charles Poletti and his officers were invited to spend many pleasurable hours eating excellent fish dishes and drinking tea. The Americans were given a warmer welcome than the British, both by the middle-class families and the poor populations. They were ready to share food and close their eyes to the petty crime caused by hunger or simple need. Poletti ruled more or less like the Roman provincial governors who demanded submission and slavishness. C. Piraino Ajello even wrote a poem, dated September 21, 1943:

> I place my trust in you, exceptional Colonel
> Enterprising and determined healer,
> That you may rebuild a more beautiful Palermo
> Like a closed flower blooming once again.
> For 22 years I was in exile
> Without help or freedom.
> This is why I ask you O great soldier
> Of the greatest nation,
> To give this people you have liberated
> Bread and security,
> Heal the wounds....
> You are the symbol of justice and freedom
> To the shame of those who wanted war.
> Sicily welcomed you with open arms
> And is grateful to you and to England,
> Strong warrior with a keen mind!
> I pray God for victory for you to free
> the tricolor flag.

Chapter 7

Allied Military Government
and the Return of the Mafia

In Allied plans the conquest of Sicily included creating an Allied Military Government in Occupied Territories, or AMG—an organization divided into various sections whose main task was to manage the administrative and political activity on the island and provide for the basic needs of the population. Palermo was the main headquarters, with branch offices in every municipality in Sicily.

The AMG's mission was to oversee the administration and its specific functions in various areas (health, legal, supplies) and use the economic resources of the areas under occupation. The AMG also had to enforce public order with the collaboration of the Carabinieri to combat several forms of criminal activity brought about by the desperate living conditions of most of the population. General Harold Alexander was in overall charge of the Allied Military Government and his deputy, Lord Francis Rennel of Rodd, acted as the hands-on administrator for the island with two high-ranking officers, Commodore C. E. Benson, head of Civil Affairs of the British Eighth Army, and Colonel Charles Poletti, head of Civil Affairs of the American Seventh Army.

There were obvious duplications and overlapping areas in the Allied administration of civil affairs in Sicily. The British referred back to their long experience at ruling many different colonies by using the principle of "indirect rule," meaning they would delegate public administration and other important social functions to local individuals who already enjoyed a certain prestige. The British therefore felt comfortable with the Italian aristocracy, which was the only class capable of playing a role in the immediate future on the island.

The Americans were more inclined to let their own officers govern the occupied territories, selecting carefully those who could speak the Sicilian dialect and giving preference to the sons of Italian immigrants. In some ways the AMG followed two systems of administration, British and American, depending upon who was in charge. Local civilian administrators selected those who could handle the most sensitive tasks. There was clearly an element of risk involved: should the choice be limited to the anti-Fascists, the problem was to identify the real ones or at the very least those who had been less enthusiastic in approving of Mussolini. There were many Mafiosi who had reappeared with the Allied landings on the island. In many cases AMG officers arrested those who had held important positions, such as prefects and podestà (mayor), while the purge of important persons among the Sicilian ruling classes who had been compromised by the Fascist regime was too often based on sketchy or superficial judgments. Rennel understood that it would be impossible to run Sicily without the old administrative staff. In twenty years of dictatorship the intermingling of the Fascist Party and public administration that could not function without the civil servants who had worked under Fascism. Therefore the appointment of people who were in black shirts only months before but who had been "forced into Fascism" became inevitable.

On July 10, a few hours after the landings, the British occupied the towns of Arola, Noto, and Pachino. Siracusa was occupied that night. The following day three AMG officers took over the administration of the city and used a few trucks for communications between the city center and the military areas. In a few days the provinces of Siracusa and Ragusa were organized with a complete Allied administration with legal, finance, and public health officers. The initial phase was marred by a dearth of transportation and personnel for the AMG in Sicily, so much so that General Montgomery, in conversation with Lord Rennel joked that if there were no trucks civil servants could use bicycles. One of the most difficult problems confronting the AMG's legal division was overcrowding in the prisons. Hundreds of prisoners were awaiting trial for political reasons. The end of the Fascist regime had prompted many requests for freedom by political prisoners. One of the worse prisons was on the island of Favignana, described in an AMG report as "a criminal penal colony where starvation was added to the horrors of awful sanitary conditions." The report continues:

At Trapani and Catania the prisons were opened indiscriminately by Allied troops and most of the detainees who were common criminals were released. It was therefore necessary to carefully examine the prison files before releasing the victims of Fascist tyranny. The work was done by the legal and security divisions and some 663 political prisoners were set free.

Among the common criminals there were also the "picciotti," (Mafia "soldiers") who were set free as a consequence of the newly proclaimed democracy. At Ustica, mixed in with political exiles of the Fascist regime, there were also criminals and some local gang leaders. Major Hickinbotham, a British intelligence officer, went there alone on a small boat and occupied the island at the end of July. Among the detainees the major found sixty-three Yugoslav civilians and nine Greeks all of them in distressingly poor condition, who told him they had been brutally tortured. Some of the men said they had not had any food in many days and that their jailers were expecting them to die of starvation. The island was living up to its historical reputation during Greek and Roman times when during the wars between Siracusa and Carthage large numbers of mercenaries were left there to die in the same way. A further investigation showed that prison officials had perpetrated a monstrous scam: "They received about twelve lire per day from the government to feed the prisoners but actually only spent two or three lire while they embezzled the rest. The prisoners who complained were cruelly tortured and died."

The AMG wanted to prosecute those responsible as war criminals. However, the investigation concluded that there was not enough evidence to try them as such, "since Italian prisoners were treated in the same manner and that it had nothing to do with the war."

The Weakness of the AMG Organization

Only seventeen AMG officers landed in Sicily on July 11, 1943, and there was a long delay in bringing in a group of another fifty officers. Only after July 28 did another group of sixty-two officers reach Palermo, which was already occupied, as well as the provinces of Trapani, Agrigento, and Caltanissetta. In the northwestern part of Sicily, American combat troops had to interact with civilian administration directly. Dealing with a hungry population that had gone through a wartime situation was no simple task, in spite of the warm welcome given to the liberators. In a letter to General Harold Alexander, Lord Rennel wrote that he believed that "the success of the AMG was based more on luck than good management." There were no instances of hostility on the part of Italian civilians toward the Allies and the warmth of the welcome given to the Anglo-American forces that had invaded Sicily was universal. This expansive sympathy of Sicilians toward American soldiers was not always spontaneous but actually reflected the influence of local Mafia leaders. It was easy to notice in the streets of Sicilian towns prior to the arrival of the Americans the presence of tough-looking individuals imparting instructions on how the population should welcome General Patton's soldiers. A love-hate relationship existed between AMG officers and the population: if, on the one hand, the Allies meant the end of hunger and suffering, on the other hand they were also the new invaders who demanded obedience and submission. It was the same old story for the Sicilian population that once again saw its land being trampled by warriors whose language it did not understand.

The cooperation between the AMG and the civilians opened up all kinds of relationships for Italian public employees where former Fascists, the police, and above all the Carabinieri, had to maintain order and enforce the law. This applied to the areas that were very antagonistic to law and order, such as the sulfur mines of Sommatino, where, as an AMG report states, the municipal buildings were occupied by a local group that proclaimed, of all things, a Communist regime.

Allied officers had to solve many different issues. Lt. Col. Gerald Wellesley, a Civil Affairs officer at Caltanissetta, summed up the AMG's tasks in a few words: "Bury the dead and feed the living." It was not just a statement because burying the dead in that hot month of July was no simple matter.

Many bodies were still trapped under the rubble and could not be extracted fast enough. There was a shortage of caskets and at times— as it happened in an inland town—the gravediggers went on strike to protest working conditions. The bodies were then piled up and burned on street corners by AMG soldiers.

Food distribution to the population was a major problem, not just in Sicily but in the rest of Italy as well until the end of the fighting in May 1945. It was dramatic during the first days of the occupation. One report states that because of the reluctance of wheat growers to bring their products to the collection centers and the rapid growth of the black market, the actual bread rations distributed by district were different during the days preceding the invasion: from 125 grams to 200 grams per person per day, while a few cities on the eastern coast were supplied for a few months from the mainland. The official ration was set at 150 grams of bread plus a weekly ration of 60 grams of pasta a day. The stores were low because the latest harvest had not yet been delivered. Actually part of the harvest was not even brought in or was destroyed in military operations. The Germans were also removing any wheat kept in storage whenever they had the time or the opportunity to do so. The reluctance on the part of the farmers to deliver their harvest was made even worse because of the requisitioning of local transportation by the two armies of occupation. All vehicles could be legitimately requisitioned and once Allied forces could no longer find any motor vehicles that the Germans had abandoned they began using mules and carts.

Lord Rennel noted in his first report on the situation in Sicily to General Alexander that on several occasions AMG officials set up columns of carts and mules. Even though they found wheat once and the means of transportation, the problem remained because the mills ran on electricity that had been cut almost everywhere during the first days following the invasion. It was therefore extremely difficult to provide for the larger and mid-sized cities.

AMG reports are a very good source for evaluating the kinds of problems the population had to confront under the occupation. The AMG official at Licata reported that the entire administration had disappeared and public utilities had ceased to function. A bomb had also destroyed the main town sewer and it was very difficult to find enough people who could repair it. He tried to assemble other workers to gather the wheat and take it to the mill. But he found out that the mill needed electric power and there was no electricity available. He therefore had to take the wheat to the nearest town, but had to use a hearse since no other means of transportation was to be had.

At Palermo the AMG was able to solve the severe food shortage because they discovered a reserve of 1,600 tons of wheat belonging to the Italian army, while at Catania the food shortage created many problems during the first weeks. Within twenty-four hours at the beginning of the occupation fifty tons of wheat were taken quickly to the town of Lentini, but the only mill that could be used was still in the area being bombed and military trucks could not be placed at risk. The wheat was therefore transferred to horse-driven wagons for the final leg of the journey. There were only 60,000 citizens still inside Catania out of its 240,000 inhabitants, but once the refugees returned the food shortage became even worse. After August 21, twenty-seven tons were required per day and three weeks later the demand reached 100,000 tons.

At Messina the food shortage was even more critical because there was no wheat grown in its area. The city had been heavily bombed and was dependent for the most part on the mainland for supplies. Due to the wartime situation it had only been receiving a daily ration of 50 grams per person. The Carabinieri were unable to stop the looting of the grain stores and the warehouses. Some looting ended in tragedy, as in Paternò where a policeman shot into the crowd, killing a child. The crowd beat and lynched the policeman who was then thrown out a window of the town hall. He was fortunate to land on some electric cables that broke his fall and only ended up having some minor injuries. All those who took part in the lynching were prosecuted and sentenced by the British military court. In the course of the proceedings no one mentioned the name of the person responsible for throwing the policeman out of the window.

Another less known but worse case took place on July 14 at Canicattì in the province of Caltanissetta and another child was to be the victim. A crowd had attacked the soap factory, Narbone-Grilli, on the viale Carlo Alberto to steal liquid soap. They were entering through a hole in the wall created by a recent bombing. An American officer, Lt. Col. George Hembert McCaffrey, was at the scene and saw some forty people inside the factory, including women and children. He asked the crowd to leave but no one listened, so he ordered his men to open fire, but they refused. He then ordered three U.S. intelligence officers to shoot. Among them was Salvatore J. Salemi, who acted as an interpreter and POW interrogator, but they also refused. Then McCaffrey took out his side arm, shooting into the crowd. A child was shot in the stomach but did not die immediately; he passed away a few days later at the local hospital. There were eight victims in all, among them a salesman who was very well known in the small town and a young farmer.

The population went hungry mostly in the larger cities. In the countryside and in the smaller towns the people were able to survive on fruits, vegetables, and nuts that were easily available. The black market was endemic in the cities and the distribution of major staples often was out of Allied control. The Sicilian Mafia had reappeared in the wake of the Anglo-American invasion as we have seen and was using the black market to make money and fill its coffers. The AMG's involvement with many Mafiosi in the socio-economic life of the island had a very negative impact and involved businesses tied to basic staples such as the transportation of salt, oil, cereals, but also so-called "luxury" goods like cigarettes and alcohol. Michele Navarra, the head of the Mafia family in the town of Corleone, set up a bus company with his brother using equipment stolen from the Allies and increased his business by getting involved in the black market. His company was purchased by the Sicilian Region in 1947. The control of the harvests was to play a key role in the Mafia's rebirth: management of huge quantities of wheat gave local bosses the control of the crowds—all they needed to do was to block or delay distribution by just one day for the population to be forced to resort to the black market as the only possible alternative to hunger.

The work of the Carabinieri did not go beyond the simple maintenance of public order, or the other police units had been corrupted by Fascism. Most police commissioners were under arrest; some remained at their posts and didn't hesitate to describe themselves as Fascists. The population had obeyed the orders to hand over all weapons but there were still many more abandoned in the countryside by Italian soldiers. These weapons were used to settle many private feuds and Mafia executions, hidden and protected by the unwritten code of "omertà." In some cases the killers were identified and put on trial, as in the murder of a landowner in the Agrigento province. The two suspects were found guilty and condemned to death by an Allied military court. In spite of the number of crimes that according to Proclamation number 2 could be punished with the death penalty, the actual number of death sentences during the entire AMG period would be insignificant, but the death sentences were all carried out without fail.

An OSS report from Palermo dated August 13, 1943, clearly describes the situation on the island. A number of shortages were expected during the coming winter unless food supplies were imported. Staples like bread and pasta, without which Sicilians could not survive, were distributed at bare minimum levels. The black market was the scourge of the shortage problem. A laborer made forty lire a day. Bread, when you could find it, was sold at 3,60 lire a kilo, but by and large the population had to buy it on the black market where the price fluctuated between 20–25 lire a kilo. Under those conditions a laborer was unable to feed his family. The black market also involved other basics and no attempt was made to do away with it: the AMG said the black market existed before the invasion and could not be eliminated. It was told to increase the price of wheat to encourage landowners to sell their harvest on the open market and benefit from larger profits, a method that the Fascist regime never used. Under Fascism when all prices were set by the government the landowner lost money and was forced into the black market; he would hide part of the harvest or refused to increase the amount of wheat he could harvest under normal circumstances. On the other hand the baker also sold his bread at a fixed price, which was sure to make him lose money, so he would also resort to selling a small amount of bread at the regular price and the rest at the black market price. The AMG increased the price of bread slightly but not enough to discourage the black market. To buy a small amount of bread people had to stand in line from the early hours of the morning until late at night. An investigation showed that bread lines began at 11 p.m.; people would stand in line until 7:30 a.m. the following morning. Men, women, and children who were too poor to buy at black market prices were kicked, pushed around, and beaten by the local police who yelled at them, "This is what you get for having applauded the arrival of the Americans!" The AMG fired seven police-men when informed of the incident.

When the OSS insisted that firing seven individuals was not enough, they recommended the elimination of all police forces because the police and the Fascist squads were the strong arm of the Fascist regime. These were the same units that consolidated Fascist power through violence, terror, and the night stick. They continued to boast how they kept law and order in the past and how the present situation required stronger tactics. Some policemen were becoming a danger to Allied military security and too used to the methods of Fascism to remain at the helm. The decision was negative: policemen could be dismissed only when specific charges were brought against them.

The Scotten Report and the Return of the Mafia

In October 1943 Colonel Bolles, the commissioner of public safety at AMG headquarters in Palermo, and deputy commissioner Lt. Col. Martin asked Brigadier General Holmes for a report on the Mafia in

Sicily. The investigation was given over to Captain W. E. Scotten, who had been U.S. vice consul in Palermo for a three-year period before the war. In his report he clearly stated that since the fall of the Fascist regime and the beginning of the American administration, the Mafia was back in control of criminal activity on the island where its presence was ubiquitous. The information contained in the Scotten report, dated October 23, 1943, came from various informers who remained unnamed to avoid jeopardizing any future action that could be decided against the Mafia or due to the sensitivity of the political aspects of the issue.

Scotten conducted an excellent and thorough investigation, enough for Bolles and Martin to agree that there the problem was urgent and had to be addressed. In his long explanation the vice consul dug into the past history of Sicily, defining it as long string of foreign invasions and occupations periodically interrupted by inadequate or authoritarian governments unable to provide internal security and more adept at ignoring rather than providing justice on the island. This was the reason why the private protection and tutelage of individuals and private property known as the Mafia appeared. Before Fascism the Mafia exercised a form of control over the political balance of power in Sicily: it could deliver elections and was courted by political parties and politicians. Even the most honest individuals who deplored this state of affairs were compelled to accept its protection. To oppose its demands and even publicize that such demands had been made meant the destruction of that citizen's property, threats and violence, or death to him or members of his family.

Cesare Mori had managed to contain the Mafia but not defeat it completely—the attack was leveled at the lowest echelons of the organization. The higher-ups were not subjected to much scrutiny except for the fact that they felt the indirect effects of the drastic measures that were taken. As Scotten wrote the Mafia was just forced to go underground under Fascism but was never totally eradicated.

A few instances of thievery and violence did take place but were never mentioned in the press. There was a lot of criminal activity controlled by the Mafia that was tolerated or overlooked by the Fascist regime. The Fascists were satisfied that the most violent aspects had been suppressed and therefore refused to admit that the Mafia still existed on the island. Everything points to the fact that since the occupation of the island and the fall of Fascism the Mafia reappeared with renewed vigor everywhere. All the offices of CIC, AMG Political Section, and the Public Safety Commissioner in Palermo were well aware of the situation.

Scotten clearly stated that the strong reappearance of the Mafia with the occupation of Sicily had serious implications for the current and future political situation on the island and in Italy itself and that the problem had to be faced very urgently. That opinion was also held by State Department special envoy Alfred T. Nester of Civil Affairs in Algiers and also a former U.S. consul at Palermo who was conducting an investigation in Sicily at the time. CIC was sending in reports that the Mafia was becoming even bolder in certain areas. Military courts had to face an increase in criminal activity. The difficulty was that to begin any investigation meant compromising sources that could become useful later on. The problem remained easy to contain at that point with quick measures. After some fifteen years the Mafia had been dormant; it had not yet regained its former strength and its organization remained relatively fragmented and the general public was not yet living in the fear and silence the Mafia usually creates so successfully. But the fear was quickly reappearing and would aggravate the problems of law enforcement. Informers had let it be known that the Mafia was obtaining the most recent new weapons and equipment abandoned on the battlefields; it was also assumed that it had large stocks of machine guns, mortars and light artillery pieces, land mines, radio transmitters and large reserves of ammunition hidden in the caves and wells near Mount Etna. The sensitive issue of the Allied relationship to the Mafia was also clear to Scotten during and following the Sicilian campaign. He pointed out that American Civil Affairs officers and interpreters of Sicilian ancestry had connections to Mafia circles in the United States through family and friends. Informers were saying how high-level officials had been sensitive to the entreaties of the landed aristocracy that had a close relationship to the Mafia, not just for traditional reasons but also because of the political aspirations they both shared. These informers insisted that U.S. officials were misled and blinded by interpreters and counselors who were corrupt or in-fluenced to the point of running the risk of becoming the unwitting instruments of the Mafia. But even if the Americans wanted to fight the Mafia, the Sicilian people were quickly losing faith in their ability to govern. Other information from CIC and Political Intelligence con-firmed those rumors that Public Safety Division officers could not deny.

Scotten's analysis also covered the dramatic issue of the black market in food supplies and the hoarding of all kinds of staples—a situation that was "made to measure" for the Mafia, which according to other information had wasted no time taking advantage of. The methods and the organization used in those bold operations were typical enough. As long as the Mafia remained free and out of control it was impossible to find wheat to purchase in the countryside, since most farms belonged to large landowners and speculators who were under Mafia protection or even owned by the Mafia, so that no one dared identify them as such. The "omertà" had effectively sealed the mouth of the peasants and the Carabinieri were either on the take or frightened through the usual methods.

Theft, the black market, the resale of foodstuffs at quadrupled prices, were part of the criminal aspects of the Mafia that became apparent as it accumulated wealth. But there was another side to organized crime that Scotten understood very clearly: in their agree-ment with the Americans, the Mafia leaders like Calogero Vizzini un-derstood the limitations of their role as a public force able to stop any type of rebellion or the impatience of the Sicilian people against the invader or politically through the democratic anointment of the god-fathers, who along with the farmers first joined the Movimento Indi-pendentista Siciliano and the Christian Democratic Party. As Scotten observed, the political significance of the Mafia could be viewed in light of its ties to the landowners. The separatist movement had the support of two groups interdependently linked by common interests: the large landowners and the Mafia. The reasons for this political soli-darity were obvious. The Sicilian people could see how the AMG was close to separatists and collaborators who appointed to official positions. For example, appointments to the posts of Prefect of

Palermo, most of the members of the provincial council, the mayor of Palermo, and so on were given to separatists. According to some sources this amounted to 80% of the AMG appointments in the area. The AMG was now thought to be not just at a disadvantage but actually being manipulated by the Mafia.

A comparison of the Allied Military Government and Fascism was being made by the Sicilian population. Since food rationing and the black market had also existed under Fascism, food rations were usually available, keeping things in check. After the invasion no rations were available and the black market for food was out of control—for example macaroni were eighty lire a kilo in Palermo on October 20, bread at forty-five lire while the official price of bread was ten lire and so on. Fascism had not completely eradicated the Mafia; by 1943 it was growing at an alarming rate and was even given favorable treatment by the AMG.

The U.S. vice consul concluded that the AMG faced three possible alternatives: a quick and direct action to bring the Mafia under control; a negotiated truce with Mafia leaders; giving up on any attempt to control the Mafia on the island and withdrawing into small enclaves that would have been protected and where the military government could function properly.

Only the first option seemed realistic to Scotten, as it responded to the declared objectives of the AMG but required a careful assessment of the ways and means available to carry it out—an action that had to happen a few days or weeks after his report was sent in. A totally secret and very detailed planning took place by adding Allied military personnel to the Carabinieri and the arrest of 500–600 leaders regardless of rank or whether or not they enjoyed political protection. They were to be deported without trial and kept in prison for the duration of the war. These measures were deemed to be sufficient to break the Mafia's back for a period of two or three years if the law enforcement agencies were consolidated and reorganized and fear of the Mafia was removed for the foreseeable future. The second possibility had fewer chances to succeed because it required absolute secrecy toward the Sicilian people on the part of AMG personnel and would depend upon the negotiator's ability to gain the confidence of the Mafia leaders and on their word of honor. An attempt to assess potential reactions became possible because the Allies' only interest in governing Sicily was tied to the war effort; they did not wish to be involved in local politics and wanted to turn over the governance to the Sicilians as soon as circumstances allowed it.

The Allies had the power to wipe out the Mafia but did not find it expedient to divert the necessary troops to carry out the action. The Mafia would have to abstain from interfering with the movement and trade of foodstuffs and other staples that the population wanted or products necessary to the war effort. These included transportation and the communications across the island, port operations, the bases that had been established and the work that had been done there. If the Mafia agreed not to interfere with AMG operations and personnel, then the Allies would not interfere with the Mafia as such, except in cases when ordinary crimes had to be punished through the Italian police and justice system. This would imply acceptance by the Allies of the principle of omertà, the only code the Mafia understood and respected. The third solution would have been seen as the least antagonistic and a show of weakness and would have been interpreted as such by the enemy; the rest of Italy and other occupied countries observing the AMG's Italian experiment. It would mean abandoning the island to the criminal element for a long time to come but it would also guarantee success.

AMG Officers Meet with Mafia Leaders

Joseph Russo, an Italo-American who headed the Palermo station of the OSS, was one of the most active officers working with the AMG. Scotten obtained a lot of information from him about organized crime in Sicily. Russo had established contact with the Mafia before coming to Sicily and confirmed as much in a televised interview some years ago: "When I arrived in Sicily and took over the Palermo office the first thing I did was to look for the criminals. Most of them were part of the Mafia and were to be valuable OSS informers." They liked the name and the fact that his father was born in Corleone, the heart of Mafia territory. Russo met the Mafia higher-ups, who wasted no time in reestablishing their gangster links. How many times did Russo actually meet with the Mafia bosses? At least once a month. They would come to see him for moral support then they would ask for tires, automobile tires. They needed them to get around and do their jobs, their charities as they referred to them. Whatever they were doing Russo never tried to find out, the AMG and the OSS used the Mafia the same way the Mafiosi tried to use us."

The AMG handed out every kind of job to big and small Mafia types. Don Calogero Vizzini, as we have seen, became mayor of Villalba; Salvatore Malta, mayor of Vallelunga; Genco Russo, super-intendent of civil affairs at Mussomeli; Damiano Lumia became the confidential interpreter (we do not know whether for the Mafia or the Americans) for the Civil Affairs office in Palermo; Max Mugnani a well-known drug smuggler, operated a warehouse for pharmaceutical products in the countryside near Cerda where the Americans had accumulated large stocks; and Mafia boss Vincenzo De Carlo was put in charge of checking the wheat harvest. Those appointments, along with the issuing of gun licenses to the "soldiers" of Calò Vizzini, were in fact the official stamp of approval by political and administrative authorities that the Mafia had always wanted.

It became a power that was not controlled or subjected to any Italian laws. Some newsreels taken near the wheat harvest show individuals who looked very much like those going and coming from the American ships anchored in front of Gela. The cap, the mustache, shirt and short tie, the serious and penetrating stare: they were the local gang leaders, the oldest "men of respect" who, by their presence and duly authorized by military government officers, were making sure that the wheat harvest was delivered in orderly fashion. They wore an arm-band imprinted with the words "Civil Affairs."

The appointment of mayors was under the direct control of the AMG head of Civil Affairs, Col. Charles Poletti, himself a rather con-troversial figure, accused of making deals with the Mafia and having facilitated its reemergence. None other than Vito Genovese, as we have seen, was acting as his private interpreter.

Poletti had his headquarters at the Delle Palme Hotel in Palermo, where he would often give parties and hold working meetings with mysterious characters connected to organized crime. Before his appointment to the AMG, Poletti had been a lawyer and a lieutenant governor of the State of New York. He was also governor for a brief two-month period in 1942. His appointment had been harshly criticized when he was lieutenant governor under Herbert Lehman— this was when the ONI was making its agreement with the New York Mafia—and a few well-known criminals had been let out of prison. Poletti signed the order to free such individuals as Francesco Gambino (serving a life sentence for murdering his cousin), Peter Tusa (life sentence for homicide), John Santapaola (thirty years for homicide), and others like Mario Pece, Maurice Buonuomo, Anthony Gerardo, and even a known racketeer, Filarginio De Pasquale, who had impersonated a medical doctor. Poletti was appointed to the AMG Civil Affairs division in April 1943 with rank of lieutenant colonel.

Even to this day in Sicily there are some who are convinced that this enterprising Italo-American (his father came from Piedmont and his mother from Bergamo) had visited the island a whole year prior to the landings and had lived secretly in the Palermo house of a lawyer close to the Mafia, where he officially worked as a butler. But these were certainly wild rumors. Poletti always denied not only all accusations of collusion with Mafia elements while he was in Sicily but also the existence of the Mafia, which he called an "intellectual invention." "We never had a problem with the Mafia," he said in an interview at age 99 in 2002. "While we were there we never heard about it because obviously they couldn't do anything while the army was everywhere." When asked whether he had met Calogero Vizzini and had appointed him mayor of Villalba, Poletti replied: "I never heard the name before. My officers were in charge of appointing mayors. Villalba? I wouldn't know where Villalba is, it can't be such an important place. I have never heard of it."

Poletti did support the separatist movement headed by Finocchiaro Aprile, who was a Freemason and all those who supported it: farmers, clients, and Mafia henchmen like Vizzini, Russo, and Navarra. With the support of the head of Civil Affairs, the Movement for Sicilian Independence could also count on Cavaliere Lucio Tasca, the main representative of the Sicilian landowners, appointed mayor of Palermo on September 27, 1943, by Col. Poletti. In December of the same year Poletti received an honorary doctorate in Political Science at the University of Palermo.

An OSS report specifically accused Poletti of being a poor administrator and even of having employed former Fascists as police-men under his orders:

> Four agents have been readmitted to the police force under Col. Poletti's orders. They had fled just before our entry into Palermo and reappeared without giving any kind of explanation. Poletti is not governing the city or the State of New York and does not understand the situation in Sicily, its population or the forces at work within local politics. As long as he is in charge he will continue to make mistakes. Instead of arresting the chief of police, the head of the security guards and the commander of the Carabinieri, all have retained their full powers. This is taking place in all the towns under our occupation except for a few villages where the Civil Affairs coordinator is working with the anti-Fascists. But even though in Palermo province and in the rest of the island everyone knows that the Cardinal had Fascist connections, he is now an advisor to General Patton.

In September 1943 Poletti decided to stop the contracts for, demolition of Palermo's bombed buildings and the removal of the rubble. The Allied daily, *Sicilia Liberata,* as newsman Franco Nicastro relates in his article "Voci e parole dalla Sicilia Liberata" in *Arrivano gli americani,* wrote: "The decision came after a number of criminal incidents" involving some organized crime figures. Citing an investigation of Mario Genco by the *Giornale di Sicilia* Nicastro explained that the

> gang of wagon masters had cornered the business, was engaged in fraud on the amount of rubble to be removed and threatened the civil engineers who were supposed to report on the work done. It was forging signatures and documents and used intimidation to rig the bidding process; stole abundantly from abandoned homes and

used the same wagons to transport the stolen goods. This was how a few wagon drivers suddenly went into the building business.

Lord Francis Rennel of Rodd also noticed the Allied-Mafia connections and who attempted to justify the decisions of his men by saying that over half of Sicily's adult population was illiterate and there was little choice among candidates for an unremunerated position in many of the smaller towns. There were few Sicilians at any level, whatever their political views, ready to work and take on responsibilities subjected to criticism by their peers. Most localities were torn by jealousies and feuds and could not agree on any names to propose. Many officers picked the loudest among the people who were proclaiming their freedom from Fascist rule or followed the suggestions of their interpreters who had learned some English during a stay in the United States. The results were not always good and the choices often went to the local Mafia boss or one of his men who had sometimes made his way among American gangsters. What could be said of these men was that they certainly were anti-Fascists but were also undesirable in every other aspect. The first days of the occupation were difficult and foreigners had little time to evaluate local characters. The Mafia, in any case, found a new legitimacy and a future to look forward to.

above

A group of peasants returning to their hometown after several weeks spent in fields to avoid Allied bombardment.

right

Enthusiastic crowds cheer American troops entering Palermo.

Boatloads of food arriving
at the port of Palermo.

POWs being processed by
AMGOT officers in Palermo.

Bread rations are distributed
to the population at Sant'Agata
di Militello near Messina.

above
Italian POWs from Sicily sent home as civilians after surrendering.

below
Italian political prisoners at Favignana
Island penitentiary.

above

The political prisoners arriving at Trapani on August 23, 1943, after being liberated by American forces.

right

Marco Barraco, the mayor of Mazara del Vallo, near Trapani, speaking to the population from the balcony of City Hall on July 28, 1943.

below

A Palermo casket maker, 1943.

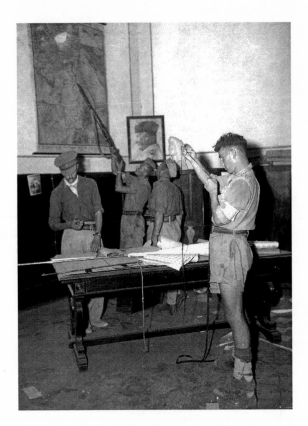

left

AMGOT officers conducting a search of Fascist Party headquarters in Catania in August 1943.

below

Joe Ballo *(center)*, an American soldier of Sicilian descent, posing for a picture with his relatives and grandparents at Gela on July 11, 1943.

above

Corporal Salvatore Di Marco, U.S. Army, also of Sicilian descent, dancing with Giuseppina, one of his cousins assembled at his grandparents' home at Mezzojuso, near Palermo, on August 3, 1943.

left

Don Vito Cascio Ferro, one of the modern founders of the Sicilian Mafia accused of murdering Joe Petrosino.

right
Don Calogero Vizzini,
Mafia leader at Villalba.

below
A rally for Communist Party
leader Girolamo Li Causi in a
Sicilian village in 1948.

above
The funeral of Don Calogero Vizzini, who died on July 11, 1954. Genco Russo *(fifth from the right)* is holding the cordon tied to the casket.

below
Genco Russo *(center)* at Mussomeli during a religious ceremony.

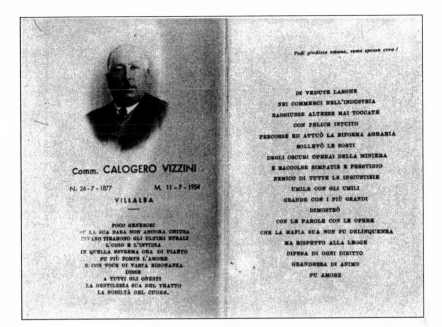

above
The obituary of Calogero Vizzini
distributed during his funeral
at Villalba.

right
Cesare Mori, known as the
"Iron Prefect," was sent to Sicily
by Mussolini to wipe out the Mafia.

above

A separatist rally in Palermo.

left

Andrea Finocchiaro Aprile, leader of MIS, the Sicilian independence movement.

below

The first photograph of the bandit Salvatore Giuliano secured by the police.

right
Salvatore Giuliano with OSS
officer Mike Stern.

below
OSS group in Palermo. *From the left in back:*
Com. Kramer; Capt. Olds, U.S.N.; Capt. Frank
Tarallo; and Mike Burke. *From the left in front:*
Com. Dufek, Lt. Col. Douglas Fairbanks, Jr., Rudy
Winnaker, Steve Martin, and Capt. Max Biagio
Corvo. The man behind Corvo is unidentified

above
Corvo *(left)* with Raimondo Craveri
and another officer.

right
Emilio Q. (Mim) Daddario.

below
Max Corvo in Palermo.

above
General William J. Donovan, head of the OSS.

left
Col. John Ricca.

below
OSS and AMGOT meeting. *From the left:* Max Corvo, Frank Tarallo, Maj. Orfeo Bizzozerro, Col. Charles Poletti, Vincent Scamporino, Maj. James H. Angleton. *Standing:* Tom Stonebrought and Vincenzo Vacirca.

above
Vincent Scamporino.

right
Sergeant Tony Ribarich

below
Earl Brennan, head of the Italian
Section of the OSS.

left
September 3, 1943, the day the Italian armistice was signed at Cassibile.
From the left: Vice Consul and interpreter Franco Montanari, Attorney Vito Guarrasi, Major Galani, and General Giuseppe Castellano. The two American officers in uniform have not been identified.

below
Colonel Charles Poletti, Head of Civil Affairs at AMGOT, receives an honorary doctorate from the University of Palermo in Law and Political Science. On the left is Prof. Giovanni Baviera, the dean of the university.

British AMGOT officers interrogate Rosario Brancati, a Catania official under the Fascist regime.

Chapter 8

Old and New Mafia

While Sicily was still occupied by Anglo-American troops under the AMG administration, and the close scrutiny of American intelligence officers, the underworld found the ideal terrain to develop its natural ability for crime and began the penetration of state agencies that started the great transformation from the old to the new Mafia. Lucky Luciano had sent some clear signals from America regarding this change, especially that the men in charge of running state entities and agencies could best be corrupted rather than killed. The way business was being conducted had to change and illegal activities as such would no longer belong to a single family but to a new organization called Cosa Nostra that would chart its course.

The arrival of the Americans was like manna from heaven for the Sicilian Mafia. Not only were its leaders appointed mayors (therefore legitimizing their exercise of power) but they were also allowed to pursue their criminal enterprises in various areas under AMG control. The Americans offered a reward for the collaboration of the bosses before and after the invasion of Sicily but also a way to combat the anticapitalist sentiments that were gaining ground among the island's most ignorant and wretched peasants. Once returned to the sovereignty of King Victor Emmanuel III and Marshal Pietro Badoglio, a liberated Sicily was therefore handed over to organized crime that was settling into public administration to govern the island and play a role as transit point for the international narcotics trade that was just about to become the main focus of the American Mafia.

Many criminals, while boasting dubious certificates of anti-Fascism, returned from internal exile where Mori had sent them years before; others returned from the United States where they had been branded as "undesirables." The lists of these former gangsters were endless and included characters who had been inmates at various American penitentiaries or were under regular FBI surveillance. These included a Mafia leader like Lucky Luciano but also lesser characters of organized crime: murderers, bodyguards, people prone to violence and who upon returning to Italy would lead a modest and unassuming life filled with the memories of New York's nightclubs and whorehouses and the homicides they perpetrated under orders from the various godfathers. At the end of the war, the United States thanked many of these criminals for the assistance they provided and at the same time wished to rid itself of their presence, even from prison. Over 500 such individuals were shipped back to Italy, permanently deported to their country of origin. Many returned penniless and survived by taking menial jobs. Some even asked for a state pension for "the work they had done overseas," but naturally they were unable to document any of it properly. In the excellent book by Giancarlo Fusco, *Gli indesiderabili,* a former gangster who had returned to Italy described his "sad" condition: "So this is the gratitude of the Americans after helping them land in Sicily? I left like a poor bastard and that's exactly how I return."

Many others entered the lucrative narcotics business that was to have one of its main hubs in Sicily during the postwar period. They also set up companies and small family businesses as fronts for other much more lucrative enterprises.

Lucky Luciano was also an "undesirable alien" but his years in exile in Italy were far more satisfactory. He had already been in jail for ten years for abetting prostitution when he was forced to return to Italy.

He had an easy time in prison, especially during the last few years when he became the main source of information and contacts for the Office of Naval Intelligence during the Underworld Project. He was the only prisoner allowed to wear a three-carat diamond ring while in jail. Other detainees had to line up in the courtyard to be able to talk to him. Federal agents took Luciano on board the *Laura Keene* on February 9, 1946, with the thanks of the U.S. government for his help in the war effort. A heavy rainstorm filled the gangster with deep sadness as he was being forced to leave a world that had given him wealth and fame. In Sicily Luciano had many friends and there was a lot to be done on that island, starting with the reorganization of the "honorable society." In America he had successfully given the Mafia a new face by transforming the old godfathers into legitimate businessmen. Now he was about to connect tightly with the old local bosses of his native land and in particular with Don Calogero Vizzini.

On board ship Luciano gave his lieutenants his final orders, as he was about to sail back to Italy. Then late at night he celebrated his newly obtained freedom. On arrival at Genoa he was met by a score of policemen and Carabinieri and taken under heavy escort to Lercana Friddi, where the fighting that had taken place three years before had left a mountain of rubble. The population greeted Luciano as if he were the Pope and people kissed his hand in the town square, calling him "Excellency"—the way they addressed landowners and Mafia bosses. The mayor had rented an entire hotel, the only one in Lercara, to be sure he would be comfortable enough. But Luciano only spent a few months in his hometown. With permission from the Carabinieri he went to live in Palermo where he saw only dismal poverty and despair. Everything was both heavily rationed and unavailable at the same time. He therefore turned to the black market business taking merchandise from military supply warehouses and reselling it. But that was just a sideshow.

Everything was temporary, as if I were having fun at a game. I didn't take it seriously. I didn't think I would be staying in Italy very long. The black market thing was only to keep my mind busy.

I was really waiting for news from Lansky about starting a new business in Cuba before returning to America.

Luciano returned to Cuba at the end of October 1946. Two months later, on December 22, at the Hotel Nacional in Havana, there was a summit of the American Mafia chiefs at which Luciano was acclaimed as a national hero and officially anointed as the head of Cosa Nostra. The bosses talked about many things that day but most of all about the narcotics business. Every one of them agreed that the drug business had to be under the new Mafia's control. The huge drug market and the related traffic from Europe to America meant millions and millions of dollars, an ocean of cash that got a rise even out of the ordinarily reserved Luciano.

The Cuban paradise of the Mafia would be the key to the drug business for many years until Fidel Castro and his Communist revolution swept the corrupt regime of Fulgencio Batista from power in January 1959. Sicily became the loading point of huge quantities of narcotics, the Mafia's new drug Eldorado, an assembly, refining, and dispatching center. Edward J. Mowery, a reporter at the *New York World Telegram,* wrote in August 1951 that Luciano was by then the main connection between Italian drug traffickers and American gangsters and how narcotics addiction had become a much bigger problem in the United States since the end of the war.

In the three years since Italy was liberated by the Allies, the United States has deported several hundred gangsters back to Italy... Most of those criminals are involved in the lucrative drug market and Luciano is heading it up.

After his return from Cuba the top boss of Cosa Nostra moved to Naples and married a beautiful dancer, Igea Lissoni. He often traveled to Sicily to visit an old friend, Chico Scimone, who owned a nightclub called La Giara. In the 1930s Scimone had been a piano player at the Copacabana, the famous Manhattan club owned by Frank Costello, where a young unknown Italo-American singer with a promising career, Frank Sinatra, would also perform. Scimone had played the piano on ocean liners from New York to Italy and back and had fond memories of those trips. A few months before he died in April 2005 at the Café Mokambo in Taormina's main square where he still played for the tourists, he confided to the author:

> I had a good relationship with Lucky. He came to Taormina quite often and spent many evenings at my club. He wasn't a very talkative man but his eyes were very convincing. At times in my younger days I would do him a few favors... Sometimes when I'd come back from the States he'd give me a few envelopes... I wouldn't open them but I thought there may have been money inside. I would hide them in the piano then I'd play and the music made everybody happy...even the officers on board ship were happy as they went on dreaming of Naples or Sicily... to dream they just had to close their eyes and that's what they did.

Chico got into trouble because of his friendship with Luciano but there was never any proof he had worked for the Mafia. He also told me of those months just before the landings in Sicily when he volunteered to help naval intelligence agents:

> I wanted to be useful for the good American cause in the fight against Fascism. I volunteered for the secret intelligence service but since my relatives lived in Taormina it wasn't possible. They didn't want people who had relatives on the island.

The new drug business that made Sicily a key player in the heroin traffic was not popular among the old Mafia bosses, who were looking at a different business: reconstruction and building bids that would fuel the real estate boom. Giuseppe Genco Russo, who became the new head of the Sicilian Mafia at the death of Calogero Vizzini in 1954, would often express his opinion on the matter. He thought that drugs could not become part of the Sicilian Mafia's regular activities because it was a business that required too many middlemen with whom he did not want to deal. Narcotics created rivalries and conflicts, scandals and a hostile public opinion, the loss of friendly relations with the authorities and—said Russo—the type of product that was not popular in Sicily. Why look for trouble when there were huge profits to be made in other areas? Furthermore, why play a dirty trick on the American friends by flooding their country with heroin when they were so friendly to Sicily and even named the Mafia bosses as mayors? But from the United States the pressure was on that Cosa Nostra could not lose a business that had been so lucrative during the Cuban years and had united the American Mafia families.

The entry of the Sicilian godfathers in the drug business was key, especially to reinforce the Mafia's power in competition with other criminal groups involved in the narcotics trade. Sicily would be a base to reroute the merchandise and as a guarantee to avoid any adulteration of the product. In spite of his old friendship with Calogero Vizzini, Lucky Luciano did not think much of the island's old Mafia, which specialized in protection shake-downs, feuds, the water irrigation racket, the fruits and vegetables market. Luciano also did not like the new Mafia because it got involved in messy post-war manipulations and complicated political and electoral struggles. It was much too noisy and was too quick to use its guns. However, as soon as he returned to Italy in 1946 Luciano began a whole series of legitimate dealings with Calogero Vizzini that included the "Fabbrica siciliana di confetti e dolciumi," a sweets manufacturing enterprise located on the Piazza San Francesco d'Assisi. The factory closed after a few months and the machines were dismantled in one night. A local newspaper had published an article saying that inside the candy there was a tiny pouch containing one or two grams of heroin.

Other Italo-American gangsters were to follow Lucky Luciano's example: Frank Coppola, deported from the United States as a major heroin dealer, set up shop in Pomezia in 1950 where he opened a factory of canned chicken stock for export; Nick Gentile, as an unpublished anti-Mafia report stated, was exporting canned sardines from the province of Agrigento to the United States; Carlos Marcello was exporting canned goods and cheese from Tunis; Gaetano Badalamenti in Hamburg was receiving and shipping canned goods and fruits and vegetables; Joseph Profaci created the Mamma Mia Import Company and Sunshine Edible Company to import jams and canned food products; his Sicilian agent, Antonino Cottone, head of the Mafia in Villabate, was murdered in August 1956 in an internal Mafia war. Giuseppe Bonnano, who was in business with Carmine Galante, was importing sardines and chicken broth; Vito Vitale was in the cheese and canned goods business; Calogero Orlando was importing canned goods for his New York stores. All this activity was hiding the vast narcotics business being shipped to the United States. The sweets, oranges, and canned foods filled with heroin were an easy way to ship the drug into the United States—like the canned anchovies, the barrels of olive oil, and the giant wheels of cheese that were hollow inside. These were old methods that had been used for centuries in Sicily by smugglers to carry gold, jewels, and clocks that were still in excellent working condition. In his book *Mafia e Droga* Michele Pantaleone wrote:

Giovanni Mira, a famous smuggler from Palermo, would ship to the United States every month boxes of canned anchovies that also contained small waterproof pouches of four kilos of heroin each. The Italian and American gangsters were dealing in olive oil, cheeses, various canned foods, jam, tunafish, and sardines in olive oil or salted; Charles Orlando began his activity by olive oil and cheese that he would also ship across the United States and moved to Kansas City, Missouri, in 1929. He traveled constantly from the U.S. to Italy, Turkey, Spain, Portugal, and Algeria. Carmine Galante and Joe "Bananas" Bonanno were also in the import business; John Bonventre was in business with Vito Vitale and traded in olive oil, cheese, and canned chicken stock from Frank Coppola's plant.

Sicily grows the world's best oranges and the fruit and vegetable export business was also a favorite to ship narcotics to America. A 1959 investigation by the Carabinieri uncovered a vast drug traffic that was using oranges filled with heroin. Every orange could carry about 100 grams. There were boatloads of the excellent fruit being shipped from Sicily to the U.S.

The Linking of Cosa Nostra and the Honorable Society

On July 11, 1954, the godfather of the Sicilian Mafia, Don Calogero Vizzini, died peacefully in his bed. The following day the Madre di Villalba church was filled with people from all walks of life: farmers, public officials, politicians, aristocrats, Carabinieri, detectives and all the members of the Honorable Society came to pay their respects. During the funeral service a sacred image with Vizzini's photograph was distributed, bearing the words of Don Totò, his brother and a priest:

> Of broad vision in business and industry he reached the highest pinnacle. With his intuition he envisioned and favored agrarian reform, improved the lot of poor miners and received sympathy and prestige for it. An enemy of all injustice, humble among the most humble, great among the greatest he demonstrated through words and deeds that his Mafia was not criminal but respected the law in defense of every right and noble sentiments. He was love.

Don Calò Vizzini was Lucky Luciano's best connection in Sicily even though the latter did not agree with the old fashioned ways of managing the Mafia because they still were much too tainted by the flashy manner in which they ran things. Luciano would become impatient when he was told that the local godfathers had their own vision of "power" that was best translated in the motto "to be in charge is better than making love." He was an extremely intelligent criminal and never had any attitudes that might offend Vizzini as an old Mafia boss. On the other hand Don Calò had shown how he could survive any change and reinforce his position in the process from collaboration with the American liberators to joining the separatist movement and later switching to the Christian Democratic Party where he was able to play a legitimate political role.

Giuseppe Genco Russo took over after Calogero Vizzini. Russo was the godfather of Mussomeli who during the war would "suggest" to Italian soldiers that they should stop fighting an enemy who was much stronger than themselves and would do better to go home to their families. Genco Russo was put on trial over ten times and acquitted on every occasion because of insufficient evidence. As soon as the Americans arrived he proclaimed his anti-Fascism and claimed that he had been persecuted by Mussolini. In 1934 a court sent him to the prison at Caltanissetta and later to Favignana in internal exile where he remained until 1938. That made Russo a bona fide anti-Fascist, paving the way for him into the Christian Democratic Party. In February 1944, just before the Allies turned over the island to Italian authorities, a court of five popular judges named by the AMG gave Russo a clean bill of health and restored his civil rights. By the mid-1950s, with Genco Russo in charge of the "Honorable Society" Sicily became the hub of the European narcotics traffic to the United States. The drugs were hidden in the underwear of the immigrants or visitors going to see their families. The double lids of suitcases, the bundles, large boxes, sacs filled with cloth and other unassuming containers were used to transport kilos of drugs and in the confusion of arrival the customs officers were unable to stop the flow.

With Genco Russo and Luciano the Sicilian Mafia was completely changed. The agrarian reforms that broke up the large estates also did away with the traditional Mafia types: the various kinds of enforcers who lived off the agricultural profits, the theft of livestock, the control of irrigation and the farmers' labor. The new Mafia was making deals in luxury hotels, in the offices of multinational corporations, and the well-appointed studies of politicians. From Naples Luciano continued to manage his business in the United States through his old Jewish friend, Meyer Lansky, the only one he trusted implicitly. In spite of the distance to New York, Luciano was able to calm the criminal excitement of the heads of the families who were always ready to start a gang war to grab more territory faster. Vito Genovese was the most impatient of them all, especially since he returned to the United States and wanted to be the top boss, eliminating Lucky Luciano himself. Other bosses like Joe Bonnano and Carlo Gambino were able to avoid any rash decisions that they knew could spell disaster.

With the death of Calò Vizzini the head of the American Mafia reached the moment when he could change the kind of relationship that existed between the Cosa Nostra and the Honorable Society.

Managing the drug market was no simple matter and Sicily took on added importance after the revolution in Cuba. On October 12, 1957, Luciano held a meeting in Palermo with heads of the American families and the Sicilian godfathers. The summit took place at the luxurious Hotel Delle Palme. From the United States came Joe "Bananas" Bonanno and his two deputies, Camillo Carmine Galante and Giovanni Bonventre, with Frank Garofalo, Joseph Palermo, Santo Sorge of the Cosa Nostra syndicate and handling relations with the Sicilian Mafia; Vito Vitale and John Di Bella. Lucky Luciano arrived from Naples, Genco Russo from Mussomeli, with then twelve un-identified individuals, and Gaspare Magaddino, head of the Mafia in Castellammare del Golfo and connected to the same family in Buffalo, New York. Other new emerging characters were also present, like Vincenzo Rimi, Cesare Manzella, Calcedonio Di Pisa, and Domenico La Fata. The bosses discussed how to improve the narcotics traffic between Sicily and the United States in view of the French competition in the refining of heroin and the new American legislation. They also decided to eliminate Albert Anastasia—which took place immediately after the Palermo meeting—and who would take over leadership of his family. The previous year, 1956, saw passage of the National Control Act by the U.S. Congress, which increased sentences for drug traffickers from five to twenty years in prison for importing into the United States and from ten years to life for smuggling, and added "conspiracy" as a crime associated with drug sales to be able to indict the highest levels of organized crime involved in the narcotics trade.

The merging of the Honorable Society and Cosa Nostra was a fact in Palermo. A new organization was born that would use the enormous American capital with the Sicilian Mafia's participation in the profits by defining its role in the business while letting the smaller units deal with local activities such as the building trades, protection, and markets. Until then the American and Sicilian Mafias had limited their connection to mutual assistance: hiding Mafiosi on the run or lending killers. The two groups had never really had common business interests or any shared investments. The Atlantic Ocean had served as a natural limit to the territories and there had never been any reasons for friction. The limitations were overcome by smuggling: the new business dried up the seas, overcame tall mountains, and became international.

Everyone was aware of the Palermo summit. People were talking about it in the streets and some were actually walking by the hotel in the hope of catching a glimpse of the leaders of the American Mafia. There was no interference by the local police. The first Italian anti-Mafia commission was very critical of the police on that occasion:

> What is surprising and remains unacceptable is the complete lack of interest in collecting information about this. It should have moved the dumbest policeman in Palermo to find out about it. But the lack of action by the police department is just the last in a long chain of inaction or inability on the part of the political authorities to combat the problem of the Mafia where not opposing it is equivalent to using it. The mention of five or twelve unknown individuals accompanying Genco Russo and taking part in the summit is of incredible superficiality. It is impossible that the police department of Palermo could be unable to identify those unknown persons before the end of the summit that was taking place in one of the main lounges of a centrally located and luxurious hotel in Palermo. This brazen demonstration of self-assuredness by the Mafia is due to the inefficiency of the public security services that the bosses understood very well how to evaluate.

At the Hotel Delle Palme the godfathers spent three days talking business and eating gourmet seafood. The waiters who were working there at the time remember the constantly smiling faces of the participants, the hooded looks, and the generous tips. One evening, as one waiter was serving a fine marsala wine to Genco Russo, he was able to hear the only pronouncement of the entire meeting that would be recorded in the police reports: "When there are too many dogs on the same bone [i.e., narcotics] better to stay as far away as possible." The Palermo summit did not produce sudden decisions but showed the need for another meeting to be held in America to improve upon the decisions reached in Sicily. Vito Genovese, who never ceased to believe in an old style kind of Mafia with a supreme leader having the last word, would organize another top-level summit at the house of Joseph Barbera at Apalachin in upstate New York. Genovese wanted to convince the American Mafia bosses to abandon the path taken by Lucky Luciano, do away with the commission, and get himself anointed as the new leader. Luciano and Meyer Lansky figured out the scheme and took action. To stop Genovese they chose a dishonorable but effective method: a leak to the New York Police Department, which burst into Barbera's house as the big gangster meeting was in progress. Some of the participants were able to get away while others were arrested and booked. Cosa Nostra then lost its anonymity. The FBI was also embarrassed and Director J. Edgar Hoover, who had always denied the existence of a centralized crime organization in the United States, had to mobilize all his agents to make up for lost time in a search for information and provide answers to aggressive news reporters. Hoover ordered some of his closest staff to prepare a study of the Mafia from inception up to the Apalachin meeting. In that thick document the relationship between the Mafia and the Allies during the Second World War, with documents from government investigations, were not mentioned. Only a few lines alluded to the issue and then only to state that during the war the Mafia was on the side of the Allies and had taken advantage of the population's misery to profit from the black market.

A few years later another leak delivered Vito Genovese to the FBI and sent him to prison after being found guilty of narcotics trafficking. Don Vito the boss died of a heart attack in a Missouri prison in 1969.

Chapter 9

The Mafia and the Allies
Against Communism

The window of Joseph Russo's room overlooked the entrance of the stately building used as the office of the Palermo section of the OSS. The Italo-American who was in charge of the local U.S. intelligence branch could see anyone entering and leaving the building. A few years ago in an interview on the BBC he remembered:

> One morning there were some civilians at the main gate when they reached the guard he asked them in Sicilian dialect, "What the hell do you want?" In Sicilian, you understand. Among them was Calogero Vizzini, who just looked at him and smiled. Then they came up the stairs to my office and sat in front of my desk asking what they could expect as Sicilians and what we intended to do about those people who were "cursed by God"—meaning the Communists. Perhaps, I asked, it would be best if we simply eliminated that word. Then I said: that we don't intend to do

anything against the Communists, since we are allies. But Vizzini looked at me straight in the eyes and said: "Commander, I don't believe you."

Vizzini was not wrong. Communism was the common enemy of both the Mafia and the Americans and once the island was occupied and Fascism eradicated the Americans needed to create a new front against the emerging Red ideology. OSS agents, who at first encountered many problems because of the poor coordination with the army and Patton's lightning advance, were diligently applying all the rules they had learned in training and establishing contacts with the same people Corvo and his group had cultivated. The Mafia that had been described by Vice Consul Scotten as an alarming and growing problem became very important for the AMG in the new political situation prevailing on the island.

A classified document dated August 13, 1943, drafted by OSS Palermo for OSS Algiers summarizing activity in Sicily, pointed out the connections with the local Mafia. The report stated that the OSS was cooperating with AMG in uncovering black market activity and, more specifically, the sale of bread to the poorest segments of the population. They also dismissed certain elements in the local police force deemed to be dangerous to the Allies. Those additional activities did not prevent regular espionage functions.

The work of Scamporino and his men to enlist so many civilians dedicated to reestablishing democracy in Italy was continuing. Italian volunteers were both eager to land on the continent and dedicated to fighting Fascism for the Allied cause. These men were ready to engage in homicide, sabotage, and to foment riots; they were intellectuals, professors, lawyers, etc. The OSS, however, had needed more good radio operators.

The report also mentioned the importance of the Mafia and how it had a bearing on intelligence operations. It always played an important role in Sicily and was divided into different factions, the top layer of lawyers and professionals and the lower level that grouped everyone else, including laborers and petty criminals. Only the Mafia could eliminate the black market and influence the peasants, who were the majority of the population. At first the OSS could only count on the Partito d'Azione—the Action Party founded in 1942 by a group of Republicans and liberal Socialists—and on the Mafia, whose leaders they met. According to the agreement the Action Party would take action on OSS suggestions and orders, and had to live up to that commitment. The Action Party provided the names of its most important leaders throughout Italy and certified that they were not in contact with any other intelligence organizations. The liberation of Sicily was the only Allied motivation and the OSS used many Action Party members as informers, a few of them refusing any form of compensation. This cooperation created an extensive, completely secret network across Sicily. Only five people knew the identity of the OSS officers at a time when no other military intelligence unit was operating nor any State Department official was gathering political information.

The OSS tightened its relationship with organized crime by using Sicilians having close Mafia connections. According to the Anti-Mafia Parliamentary Commission one of these was Palermo attorney Vito Guarrasi, a former Italian army captain and a man of many parts. Guarrasi was a frequent visitor to the offices of Joseph Russo and was thought to be the right-hand man of General Giuseppe Castellano. He was present with Castellano and the interpreter, Vice Consul Franco Montanari, on the day the armistice was signed at Cassibile. The photograph demonstrates the Palermo lawyer's participation in the negotiations for Italy's surrender and reopens the issue of his presence in Algiers in May 1943 to discuss landing operations with Scamporino, handing him a list of Mafia contacts who could help with the invasion of Sicily. There has never been any proof that Guarrasi had ties to the Mafia, even though in a letter to the U.S. ambassador to Rome, the American consul in Palermo stated that he had a document proving that a meeting of the Mafia bosses of Sicily's three western provinces took place at the lawyer's home in Palermo. Guarrasi denied this fact in a rare interview while admitting having met Calogero Vizzini in the past.

An OSS report from the end of 1943 described Sicily's dramatic social situation: a population in the grips of all the problems created by the war and, seemingly, to be ready to explode in "insurrection." A social conflict existed that could detonate any day into riots or even revolution. The population had been oppressed for some twenty years and in the course of the war had to deal with shortages of essential items like bread, pasta, oil, soap, and clothing. The cities were almost completely destroyed and many villages were reduced to rubble. Thousands of people had lost their homes and suffered from malnutrition. Epidemics were rampant in many areas. No one was governing the various communities, while the old Fascist authorities were still in place—contrary to what was originally planned. The result was that the liberators were losing their prestige on a daily basis. The favorite expression was "For every Fascist who leaves another one shows up."

The OSS officer writing at the time also noticed how the AMG was involved in local affairs, confirming how U.S. intelligence was playing a role behind the scenes in the complicated story of postwar Italy. The continued presence of elements connected to the Fascist Party and regime within the top public institutions—prefects, police chiefs, local leaders—was part of a deliberate choice made by the Allies in a specific plan to create conservative coalitions to oppose the left-wing political parties, especially the Communists and the labor movement. This was when the so-called "ghost armies" appeared, armed by the Americans to suppress Communist agitators at labor rallies, extremist politicians, various protesters, and peasants and enforce law and order. It was then that EVIS—Volunteer Army for the Independence of Sicily—the armed unit of the independence movement made its appearance. The Salvatore Giuliano gang, helped by James Jesus Angleton's[27] counterintelligence unit, was operating while General Castellano's repression of peaceful demonstrations occurred in Palermo, when the Italian army opened fire in the Via Maqueda killing 24 and wounding 158 people. At Comiso there were 19 dead civilians and 15 soldiers; the Mafia intimidated Communist politician Girolamo Li Causi during a rally in the main square at Villalba in front of Calogero Vizzini, who applauded the shots fired by his men and by a few Fascists. The case was well known and Michele

---

27. Angleton's father was Maj. James H. Angleton of the OSS in Italy.

Pantaleone was an eyewitness, since he shared the rostrum with Li Causi.

On September 19, 1944, the square of Villalba, which was off limits to Socialists and Communist, was oddly deserted. Sitting at a table of the only café in town and surrounded by a few tough guys, Don Calò welcomed the two men with a sly and threatening smile. Pantaleoni remembered:

> He asked whether he could have the honor of offering us a cup of coffee and once we were at the counter he said very carefully, "Villalba is quiet, as quiet as a nunnery. If you really want to hold the rally, at least tell the speakers that they should know what to say."

Li Causi was the most popular Communist political figure in Sicily and his speeches moved many poor people: "On the dais at the sound of his voice, the frightened peasants who had been hiding moved on an impulse into the square where Li Causi improvised a speech to the small crowd about the Mafia and the land. The church bells suddenly began to ring, pulled by the priest, Don Calò's brother, to cover Li Causi's voice. The peasants kept on listening and understood the points he was making. "What he's saying is right, blessed be the milk that fed him, his words are Gospel." It was their way of breaking up an ancient servitude by disobeying the law of the powerful, thereby destroying authority by denigrating its prestige. It was then that Don Calò came into the square and cried out "It's not true!" and the Mafiosi began shooting. Fourteen people were wounded, including Li Causi, who was shot in the knee.

Don Calò rejected the idea that he was behind the incident but three trials concluded that he was and those who had fired the shots were also found guilty. In January 1957, three years after the Mafia's leader's death, the Italian Supreme Court was to issue its final judgment. President Giovanni Gronchi paradoxically pardoned all the other defendants in spite of the fact that they still had to serve time in jail for other crimes.

There was never any proof that Fascists had been present in the square at Villalba but it is plausible that persons unknown were also shooting against Li Causi that day. The Mafia would never threaten a politician in such a spectacular way, letting the victim live and drawing the attention of the authorities to the town. The existence of a plan to upend the social order becomes plausible with the deep mystery that engulfed Sicily at the time and led to the May 1947 shootings at Portella delle Ginestre. That shooting was attributed to Salvatore Giuliano and his gang and other individuals said to be smoking American cigarettes, according to the butts found by the farmers at that location.

An OSS report dated April 5, 1945, entitled "The Mafia Leadership Fighting Crime" describes how the Mafia was fighting banditism in the Sicilian countryside and especially along the roads and highways. The report is filled with troubling details, and a list of murders that were deemed necessary to reestablish law and order and had been approved of by the authorities.

At the beginning of March, according to the report, the Mafia leadership in Palermo held a number of secret meetings to end the crime wave. A gang of eight men was wiped out on March 5 and their bodies were found near Mussomeli at the village of Fiume Salina Nera at Cannitello. They had been shot numerous times, strangled, and burned; on March 9 the bandit Ignazio Giammanco was killed in the area of Monte Gallo near Palermo; on March 6 Giovanni Casarino and Arturo Coglitore were murdered at San Giuseppe Jato; on March 12 Biagio Bucaro was killed at Altavilla Milicia; on March 12 the body of Calogero Prizzi, a wanted criminal and a member of the Mangione gang, was found at Serradifalco near Caltanissetta. His body was burned and difficult to identify. It is thought that he took part in the kidnappings of Arcangelo Cammarata and Francesco Baglio; on March 12 Giuseppe Renda was murdered at Salemi near Trapani; on March 22 Vincenzo Dioguardi, Carmelo Leta, and a third unidentified man were shot because they had attacked the bus between Montemaggiore and Termini; on March 22 Niccolò Sciacca was killed at Petrosino near Trapani; on March 24 a man known as Monachello was killed on the road between Bresciano and Cappella degli Angeli near Castelvetrano;

on March 27 Paolo Rotolo, one of three gang leaders near Campobello di Licata, Naro and Montechiaro, was shot to death at Campobello, near Agrigento; on March 27 Giovanni Vitali was found dead at Raffadali near, Agrigento; on March 20 Antonino La Sala was eliminated at Montevago near Agrigento.

The Mafia leader Calogero Vizzini was quoted as saying:

Enough! Sicily wants peace and quiet in the countryside and on the roads. Some elements have already been eliminated but one hundred more must also fall. Fascism had insulted Sicily with its public safety laws. We were thought of as a penal colony. The Prefect Mori and his agents are responsible for the moral, political, and economic decay of Sicily. But today, the Americans can see that the island is the jewel of the Mediterranean.

The report concludes with a few rather disturbing words:

The Carabinieri and other public safety agencies were openly favorable to the Mafia leadership's interest in enforcing respect of the law and were avoiding any investigation into the killings of wanted criminals.

There was complete socio-political chaos in Sicily right after the landings. The AMG had barely handled the urgent needs of the population and had to deal with the spread of banditism, which was instilling fear in the population. The Mafia turned out to be the only well organized and coherent force able to stop the disorder that gripped Sicily. This was very clear to General Giuseppe Castellano who after having conducted the negotiations for Italy's surrender became the Italian general whom the Americans preferred to deal with to solve the deep problems of the island. On December 6, 1944, Castellano met with the Tasca brothers, Alessandro, Lucio, and Paolo, all separatist leaders and top members of the Mafia. He asked them to help keep law and order and peace on the island. The Tasca brothers agreed—if bread and pasta could be distributed to the population. Castellano, who was also a Freemason, was actually setting in motion his plan to regroup the separatists, the Mafia, and the farmers in a single unbeatable power base. The general had met with Calogero Vizzini one month before and together they talked with Virgilio Nasi, the head of the well-known Nasi family in Trapani, and asked him to lead a movement in favor of Sicily's autonomy with Mafia support. In January 1945, at a meeting with U.S. Consul Alfred Trevell Nester, Castellano explained how he also wanted to involve the CLN—the Committee of National Liberation. The Mafia, the separatists, and the CLN were collectively the only group capable of reestablishing law and order in Sicily. An OSS report signed by Vincent Scamporino, head of SI (secret intelligence), summed up the main points of the meeting:

> The general tried to promote a temporary agreement between the CLN and the MIS [independence movement] to solve the problems of Sicily and deal with the political and economic emergency by the leaders of a mass movement. Those groups support the separatists and not the leaders of the CLN and the "friends"—meaning the chivalrous old Mafia that is mostly separatist. The general thought that Sicilians would follow a leader rather than a political party. Sicilians will forget about violence and rally around a strong man.

The Mafia held a number of secret meetings in Palermo and met with Castellano on three occasions to examine the possibility of reaching an agreement with the separatists and the political parties in the CLN. But this was not very likely, since MIS leader Finocchiaro Aprile had refused to negotiate with any representatives of the Italian government that also included the CLN. Alessandro Tasca, a Mafia separatist leader, agreed but his brother Lucio Tasca the former mayor of Palermo, refused. General Castellano was still convinced that the old system of the Mafia that had been respected for centuries had to be reestablished to handle banditism and anarchy, which were spinning out of the control of the army and the police. But the old well-honed methods were no longer promoted by the Mafia.

Calogero Vizzini understood that all the summary executions and murders and the continued use of violence would lead to the dismissal of Salvatore Aldisio, the High Commissioner for Sicily, and his replacement by an army general.

Should that happen the Mafia is convinced that any riots would be followed by a state of siege. It would be an insult to the Sicilian people and the principles of freedom that the people crave after twenty years of Fascist dictatorship. The Mafia thinks that the army generals, a high military caste, are tied to the Monarchy and will only support the cause of the treacherous dynasty.

In that case the Mafia would have been forced back underground or removed its leaders from the legitimate power structures and public administrations where the Communists would have found freedom of action and jobs. The Mafia leaders were just as fearful as the Americans and the Christian Democrats, who viewed all the political forces under the Communists, including the labor groups of the CGIL, as the enemies of democracy. The violence and intimidation against the left-wing parties did not stop with its epilog after the victory of the Popular bloc at the elections of April 20, 1947, and the killings of Portella delle Ginestre. There was still a lot of violence on the island, confirming that no left-wing group could take power, even if it won the elections.

Following the landings in Sicily the alliance with the United States was necessary and a liberated Italy naturally joined the West. The only outlet for the Left was in parliamentary opposition.

The crisis of De Gasperi's third government in May 1947 and the departure of the Communists and Socialists from the executive branch opened an era of centrist governments having neo-Fascist and American support. The Mafia returned to its old ways with impunity, a feeling of invincibility. In 1944 Calogero Vizzini had already decided to support the Christian Democratic Party.

As the Anti-Mafia Commission Report states:

That party [the Christian Democrats—DC] understood down to its provincial and local branches the support its leaders could count on from Calogero Vizzini and therefore it accepted the Mafia within its ranks. At Villalba almost the entire Mafia membership joined the DC; at Vallelunga Lillo Malta joined the DC with his entire group: the Madonias, the Sinatras, etc; the Cammarata group also went over to the DC. At Mussomeli Genco Russo and his followers took over the DC in the area.

The Mafia was no longer an instrument for the defense of feudal privilege, or even the criminal enterprise it had become at the end of the last century and at the beginning of the Fascist era. In the words of Michele Pantaleone:

> In the political, economic and military reality that followed the occupation of the island by the Allies and the ideological struggle of the 1940s and 1950s, the Mafia became the extreme Fascist-type barrier to the advance of the Left in Sicily and turned the island into a bridge for gangster-type activities from the Middle East, Europe, the U.S., Canada, and Mexico.

Joseph Russo, reminiscing about those times of occupation of the island and what had taken place in the OSS offices in Palermo, concluded in his BBC interview:

> There's nothing more I can say other than what happened was very wrong. We didn't do our job. That I can tell you.

Bibliography

Ame, C., *Guerra segreta in Italia: 1940–43*, Rome, Casini, 1954.

Ardemani, S., *L'Italia e la Guerra*, Rome, 1944.

Attanasio, S., *Gli anni della rabbia: Sicilia 1943–1947*, Milan, 1984.

——, *Sicilia senza Italia: luglio-agosto 1943*, Milan, 1976.

Bartolone, G., *Le altre stragi*, Palermo, 2005.

Ball, E. F., *Staff Officer with the Fifth Army*, New York, 1958.

Biagini, A., *1 gennaio 1943–7 settembre 1943*, Rome, Uff. Storic. SME, 1987.

Blumenson, M., *The Patton Papers, vol. II*, Boston, 1974.

Boano, G., Varvelli M., *Franco Montanari, biografia*, Moncalvo, 1995.

Bradley, O. N.-Blair, C., *A General's Life*, New York, 1983.

Breuer, W. B., *Drop zone Sicily, July 1943*, San Rafael, 1983.

Brown, D.- Wagg, A., *No Spaghetti for Breakfast*, London, 1943.

Campbell, R., *The Luciano Project*, New York, 1977.

Canevari, E., *La guerra italiana: retroscena di una disfatta*, Roma, 1948.

Caruso, A., *Da cosa nasce cosa. Storia della mafia dal 1943 ad oggi*, Milan, 2002.

——, *Arrivano I nostri*, Milano, 2004.

Casarrubea, G., *Storia segreta della Sicilia*, Milan, 2005.

Castellano, G., *Come firmai l'armistizio di Cassibile*, Milan, 1945

Cave Brown, A., *Wild Bill Donovan: The Last Hero*, New York, 1982.

——, *The Secret War Report of the OSS*, New York, 1976.

Chalou, G. C., *The Secret War*, Washington D.C., 2002.

Chandler, A. D. (ed.), *The Papers of Dwight David Eisenhower: The War Years, 5 Vols.*, Baltimore, 1970.

Ciano, G., *Diario 1939–43*, Milano, 1946.

——, *Diario 1937–1943 (a cura di Renzo De Felice)*, Milan, 2000.

Clarke, J. W., *American Assassins*, Princeton, 1982.

Cole, D., *Rough Road to Rome: A Foot-Soldier in Sicily and Italy (1943–44)*, London, 1983.

Corvom, M., *The OSS in Italy, 1942–1945. A personal memoir*, N.Y., 1990.

Costanzo, E., *L'estate del '43. I giorni di guerra a Paternò: foto, documenti e testimonianze*, Catania, 2001.

——, *Sicilia 1943. Breve storia dello sbarco alleato.* Catania, 2003.

Darby, W., *Darby's Rangers: We Led the Way*, 1980.

De Felice, R., *Breve storia del fascismo*, Milan, 2002.

De Risio, C., *Generali, servizi segreti e fascismo: la guerra nella guerra, 1940–1943*, Milan, 1978.

D'Este, C., *1943, Lo sbarco in Sicilia*, Milan, 1990.

Duggan, C., *La mafia durante il fascismo*, Catanzaro, 1986.

Dolfin, G., *Con Mussolini nella tragedia: diario del capo della segretria particolare del duce, 1943–44,* Milan, 1949.

Eisenhower, J. D., *Allies, Pearl Harbor to D-Day,* New York, 2000.

Ellwood, D., *L'alleato nemico. La politica dell'occupazione anglo-americana in Italia 1943–1946,* Milano, 1977.

Faenza, R.-Fini, M., *Gli americani in Italia,* Milan, 1976.

Faldella, E., *L'Italia nella seconda guerra mondiale,* Rocca S. Casciano, 1959.

——, *Lo sbarco e la difesa della Sicilia,* Rome, 1956.

——, *L'Italia nella seconda Guerra mondiale: revisione dei giudizi,* Bologna, 1959.

Feder, S.-Joesten, J., *The Luciano Story,* New York, 1994.

Finkelstein, Monte E., *Separatism, the Allies and the Mafia,* London, 1998.

Franzinelli, M., *Guerra di spie,* Milan, 2004.

Frediani, G., *La pace separata di Ciano,* Rome, 1990.

Fusco, G. C., *Gli indesiderabili,* Palermo, 2003.

Garland, A. N.-McGaw Smyth, H., *Sicily and the Surrender of Italy,* Washington, 1965.

Giarrizzo, G., *Roma-Bari,* Catania, 1986.

Gosh, M.-Hammer, R., *L'ultimo testamento di Lucky Luciano,* Milan, 1975.

Harris, C.R.S., *Allied Military Administration of Italy 1943–1945,* London, 1957.

Hinsley, F. N., *British Intelligence in the Second War,* London, 1979.

Jannuzzi, L.-Rosi, F., *Lucky Luciano,* Milano, 1973.

Isgró, P.-Nicolosi, C., *Labari e campanili,* Catania, 1982.

Kefauver, E., *Il gangsterismo in America,* Milan, 1959.

Kesselring, A., *Memorie di guerra,* Milan, 1954.

Keegan, J., *La seconda guerra mondiale 1939–1945. Una storia militare,* ed. It., Milan, 2002.

Klinkhammer, L., *Stragi naziste in Italia,* Rome, 1997.

Lacey, R., *Little Man,* Boston, 1991.

Lamb, R., *La guerra in Italia, 1943–1945,* Milan, 1996.

Linklater, E., *The Campaign in Italy,* London, 1951.

Liotta, C., *L'invasione della Sicilia,* Augusta, 1973.

Leonardi, D. U., *Luglio 1943 in Sicilia,* Modena, 1947.

Lewis, N., *The Honoured Society,* New York, 1964.

Lupo, S., *Storia della mafia dalle origini ai giorni nostri,* Rome, 1993.

Lumia, L., *Villalba, storia e memoria,* Caltanissetta, 1990.

Maltese, P., *Lo sbarco in Sicilia,* Milan, 1981.

Mangiameli, R., *La mafia tra stereotipo e storia,* Caltanissetta, 2000.

Mangiameli, R., (a cura di), *Sicily Zone Handbook, 1943,* Caltanissetta, 1994.

Marino, G. C., *I padrini,* Rome, 2001.

——., *Storia della mafia,* Rome, 1998.

——, *Storia del separatismo siciliano: 1943–1947*, Rome, 1979, 2. ed. 1993.

Marcon, T., *Assalto a tre ponti, da Cassibile al Simeto*, Siracusa, 1993.

——, *Augusta 1940–43: cronache dalla piazzaforte*, Rome.

Mercuri, L., *La quarta arma. 1942–1950: propaganda psicologica degli Alleati in Italia*, Milano, 1998.

Miccinesi, M., *Tra mine e siluri: nel canale di Sicilia*, Milano, 1975.

Mosca, G.-Caselli, G. – Ingroia A., *Che cosa è la mafia*, Bari, 2002.

Montgomery, *Memoirs*, London, 1960.

Nicastro, F.-Mangiameli., *Arrivano...Gli americani a Vittoria nel l'estate del '43*, Vittoria, 2003.

Nicolosi, S., *La Guerra a Catania*, Catania, 1983.

——, *Sicilia contro Italia: il separatismo siciliano*, Catania, 1981.

O'Donnel, P. K., *Operatives, Spies and Saboteurs*, New York, 2004.

Ollar, R., *Padrini*, Milan, 2003.

Overy, R., *La strada della vittoria. Perché gli Alleati hanno vinto la seconda guerra mondiale*, ed. It., Bologna, 2002.

Pantaleone, M., *Mafia e politica*, Turin, 1978.

——, *Mafia e droga*, Turin, 1979.

Pantaleone, M., *A cavallo della tigre*, Palermo, 1984.

Passalacqua, A., *Contributo alla Storia. La Verità sulla difesa di Catania*, Rome, 1956.

——, *La difesa della Sicilia*, Rome, 1956.

Paternó Castello, F., *Il movimento per l'indipendenza della Sicilia: memorie del duca di Carcaci*, Palermo, 1977.

Petacco, A., *Il prefetto di ferro*, Milan, 1976.

Powell, H., *Lucky Luciano*, New York, 2000.

Rossi, A. E., *Una nazione allo sbando. L'armistizio italiano del settembre 1943*, Bologna, 1998.

Renda, F., *Storia della Mafia*, Palermo, 1997.

Rennel of Rodd J., *The Italian people*, London, 1920

Rossi, F., *Come arrivammo all'armistizio*, Milan, 1946.

Santoni, A., *Le operazioni in Sicilia e in Calabria (luglio-settembre 1943)*, Stato Maggiore dell'Esercito, Ufficio storico, Rome, 1983.

Senato Della Repubblica V legislature, doc. XXIII n. 2, sexies, Commissione parlamentare d'inchiesta sul fenomeno della mafia in Sicilia, *Relazione sui rapporti tra mafia e banditismo in Sicilia*.

—— n. 2, quarter, Commissione di inchiesta sul fenomeno della mafia in Sicilia (legge 20 dic. 1962, n. 1720), presidente Franco Cattanei, *Relazione sull'indagine riguardante casi di singoli mafiosi*, Rome, Tip. Colombo, 1972.

—— n. 2, septies, Commissione parlamentare di inchiesta sul fenomeno della mafia in Sicilia (legge 20 dic. 1962, n. 1720), presidente Franco Cattanei, *Relazione dei lavori svolti e sullo stato del fenomeno mafioso al termine della v legislatura, approvata nella seduta del 31 marzo 1972,* Rome, Tip. Colombo, 1972.

—— n. 2, Commissione parlamentare d'inchiesta sul fenomeno della mafia in Sicilia (legge 20 dic. 1962, n. 1720), *Relazione conclusiva, relatore Carraro – Relazione sul traffico Mafioso di tabacchi e stupefacenti nonché sui rapporti tra mafia e gangsterismo italo-americano: relatore Zuccalà – Relazioni di minoranza: 1) relatori La Torre e altri: 2) relatori Nicosia e altri; communicate alle Presidenze delle Camere il 14 febbraio 1976,* Rome, Senato della Repubblica, 1976.

Spinelli, F. A., *Perché esiste il mercato nero?,* Milan, 1942.

Sprigge, C. J. S., *Il drama politico dell'Italia,* Rome 1945.

Strawson, J., *The Italian Campaign,* London, 1987.

Taylor, A. J. P., *Storia della seconda guerra mondiale,* ed. It., Bologna, 1990.

Tranfaglia, N., *Mafia, politica e affari,* Rome-Bari, 2001.

——, *Come nasce la Repubblica,* Milan, 2004.

Toscano, M., *Dal 25 luglio all'8 settembre,* Florence, 1966.

Whiting, C., *Slaugther over Sicily,* London, 1992.

Zingali, G., *L'invasione della Sicilia, 1943: avvenimenti militari e responsabilità politiche,* Catania, 1962.

Index